The Fullness of the Holy Spirit

Introducing Christian Spirituality

The Fullness of the Holy Spirit

Introducing Christian Spirituality

Sung Min Jeong

Tercentenary Publication
2010

The Fullness of the Holy Spirit- Published by the Rev. Dr. Ashish Amos of the Indian Society for Promoting Christian Knowledge (ISPCK), Post Box 1585, 1654, Madarsa Road, Kashmere Gate, Delhi-110006.

© Author, 2010

All rights reserved. No part of this book may be reproduced or transmitted in any form or by any means, electronic, mechanical, photocopying, recording, or by any information storage and retrieval system, without the prior permission in writing from the publisher.

The views expressed in the book are those of the author and the publisher takes no responsibility for any of the statements.

ISBN: 978-81-8465-104-1

Laser typeset by
ISPCK, Post Box 1585, 1654, Madarsa Road, Kashmere Gate, Delhi-110006 • *Tel:* 23866323
e-mail: ashish@ispck.org.in • ella@ispck.org.in
website: www.ispck.org.in

Contents

Foreword I vii
Foreword II ix
Preface xi
Prologue xiii

Chapter - 1	Follow the Holy Spirit	1
Chapter - 2	In the midst of strains of faith and environment	19
Chapter - 3	What does the Holy Spirit do?	32
Chapter - 4	How can we tell we are filled with the Holy Spirit?	37
Chapter - 5	Finding your potential gift	46
Chapter - 6	Seeking gifts of the Holy Spirit	61
Chapter - 7	Bearing the fruit of the Holy Spirit	98
Chapter - 8	In the front line of spiritual war	105
Chapter - 9	What interrupts the fullness of the Holy Spirit?	122

| **Chapter -10** | Keeping the fullness of the Holy Spirit | 137 |
| **Epilogue** | | 146 |

Foreword I

The book *Fullness of the Holy Spirit* by Dr. Sung Min Jeong is a very down-to-earth and practical book written out of the author's personal experience, conviction and study of God's word. His concern that, "some know about the Holy Spirit theoretically but it seems that they are not walking along with the Spirit throughout their lives" has led him to tackle this very crucial subject on the Holy Spirit and the need for Christians to walk under the guidance of the Holy Spirit. In short, all those who long for a victorious Christian life should not neglect the Holy Spirit, the best gift from God.

Dr. Sung Min Jeong is a thinker, scholar, writer and a missionary statesman and above all a man guided by God, the Holy Spirit. His missionary journey has taken him to various countries in South America, North America and even closed doors of Gulf countries. After dealing with the Scriptural Mandate on the Holy Spirit, the author stresses the importance of role of the Bible, in listening to God's voice in our day-to-day life. And then he stresses the aspect of prayer as an interactive channel in communicating with God, the Holy Spirit.

The author has a clear understanding of the Holy Spirit as to His functions. The author affirms that the gift of the Holy Spirit is real and is available for all those who sincerely seek them. The writer exhorts all those who seek the fullness of the Holy Spirit to have the spirit of repentance and forgiveness, and learn to live in accordance with God's word

After reading Dr. Jeong's book on the Fullness of the Holy Spirit, I am fully convinced that he is not only an intellectual, a Theologian, an Apologist and a Writer but he is also a man of God fully guided by Holy Spirit. I count it as an honour to write this foreword to his book.

I have decided that all of our 3000 ECI Pastors, Evangelists and Missionaries and Thousands of Elders and several thousands of our ECI elders and believers should read this book and form study circles and carefully learn this book chapter by chapter. I recommend this book not only for ECI readership but to other God's children everywhere to read the book and be benefited and blessed.

Chennai
December 29, 2009.

M. EZRA SARGUNAM
Bishop-President
Evangelical Church of India

Foreword II

Christians confess through the Nicene Creed that:
... We believe in the Holy Spirit, the Lord, the giver of life,
who proceeds from the Father and the Son.
With the Father and the Son he is worshiped and glorified.
He has spoken through the prophets. ...

Christian Church believes that the Holy Spirit calls, gathers, enlightens and sanctifies people in the faith, and that all of this flows from what we understand to be the Holy Spirit's paramount work — to reveal and glorify Christ, and to strengthen the believer's faith. The Spirit's activity is not limited to the sphere of faith and the church, but that all activity in which God engages with reference to the world and humankind is mediated through the Spirit. The reformer Martin Luther points out that, a true relationship with God is possible only through the Spirit, the third person of the Trinity. He believed that the activities of the Spirit are personal in nature: speaking, bearing witness, and uniting believers with one another in one body. Apart from the Spirit there is no activity of God in the world or in human life, no living Word, no grace of Baptism, no real presence of the Lord in the Eucharist, no conversion or regeneration, no faith or fellowship in Christ. Hence Luther believed that there is not a single theological doctrine in which the activity of the Spirit is not fundamental.

Dr. Sung Min Jeong's book, "The Fullness of the Holy Spirit", expounds his understanding of the spirituality in terms of life filled with the Spirit of God, through his reading of the Scripture and his life experiences. The ten chapters of the book deals with listening to the Spirit of God in the midst of difficulties that could even test our faith, seeking the gifts of the Holy Spirit and bearing the fruit of the Spirit and finally he also deals with what interrupts from being filled with the Spirit of God and tells us with his life experience the being filled with the Holy Spirit is not a one time act, but it is an on-going process, living with God in Christ through seeking forgiveness through repentance and being people of prayer nurtured through the Word of God.

It is not a book for doctrinal reading, but a book for spiritual nurture to grow in authentic spirituality experiencing the life filled with the Holy Spirit. I will not say that this book is only for the people with Charismatic or Pentecostal experience, but I this is the book everyone should read to know how the life of a person with a life filled with Spirit be. I appreciate and congratulate Dr. Sung Min Jeong for taking time to share with the readers his experience of being filled with the Holy Spirit, to glorify God and live a life worthy of God's calling, because as Luther says, the activities of the Spirit are personal in nature, speaking, bearing witness, and uniting believers with one another in one body.

Rev. Dr. Samuel W. Meshack
Principal
Gurukul Lutheran Theological College & Research Institute
Chennai, Tamilnadu, India

Preface

Written by Dr. Sung Min Jeong, the book *The Fullness of the Holy Spirit* has the power to change the reader's life. The Scriptures continually highlight the importance of being full of the Holy Spirit, yet many of us do not really know much about the Holy Spirit. Should we regard the Holy Spirit as a mystical being or a mysterious theological entity?

Using the Scriptures and illustrations, Dr. Jeong seeks to open our eyes to what he sees: a life lived in the presence of the Spirit, a life of transforming power and a life of delighting in Him. If you want to lead a vibrant spiritual life, if you want to break from the shallow Christian routine for reaching God and if you want to learn more about the Holy Spirit and feel the Spirit's presence in your life, then this book is for you. I would recommend this book not only to those who want to experience more of the Holy Spirit in their lives, but also to my God-seeking fellow ministers.

In His service,
Rev. D. Mohan
Senior Pastor, New Life AG Church in Chennai

Prologue
The Holy Spirit-the best gift from God

One day a fellow believer came and asked me a question: "How do I discern the will of God? If I can clearly know about God's will, I will give all my life to Him." I was flustered by his unexpected question. I did have my own way to discern the will of God, but it was not easy to explain it to him. It was because the answer was related to the Holy Spirit. It is unwise to explain God's voice to a person who has not yet experienced the Holy Spirit. But I wanted to say something about how to listen to the voice of God.

Many believers do not know or have misunderstandings about the Holy Spirit. Some of them know about the Holy Spirit theoretically but find it difficult to walk along with the Spirit for a long time. It is not an exaggeration to say religious life is about living with the Holy Spirit. But what do we have to do if we do not know anything about the Holy Spirit?

God promised us that he will pour the Holy Spirit on us. So, as he promised, the Holy Spirit works in all Christians. Following the Holy Spirit amounts to believing in Jesus, obeying God and, consequently, being blessed. We should try to please the Spirit and be wise in choosing things that would please the Spirit. That is why we need the ability to discern spiritually.

We need to know how we can be fully anointed with the Holy Spirit. Also, we have to learn how to use the gifts of the Holy Spirit properly. And, of course, we must bear the fruit of the Holy Spirit; that is, God's will for the church. Believers have to develop their ability to listen to the voice of God.

Through this book, I want to tell you about the Holy Spirit that has been speaking to me and guiding me through every moment of my life. I will also talk about the Holy Spirit in the light of theology and of experiencing Him in church communities. You will also find practical and detailed suggestions on how to get healthy, how to acquire sound theological knowledge and how to accompany the Holy Spirit in family and church.

So, step into the mysterious world of the Holy Spirit if you want to fervently believe in Jesus. Remember that the key to leading a happy life lies in meeting the Holy Spirit in person.

Chapter 1
Follow the Holy Spirit

Crossroads of never-ending choices

Our life is made up of a series of choices. We have to choose our spouse, job, school and church. When it comes to making a decision, we start by making the best choice. So, we have a hard time when many options are open to us.

What is the right choice? What kind of selection pleases God? Things will get much easier if we know what to select beforehand. What is the best choice for someone who believes in Jesus Christ? It may be a choice that observes God's will. But what really is God's will?

How can we discern the will of God? God gives us an insight into His will (Ps. 32:8). He is the shepherd and we are his sheep. The sheep have to listen to the voice of the shepherd and the sheep know the shepherd's voice (Jn. 10:14-15). If you are a child of God, then you should be able to listen to God's voice (Jn. 10:27).

God has His will and plan for every moment of our life. He wants us to make decisions that please Him. And then he speaks to us. Most believers say that God is not speaking to them or that they cannot hear God's voice. Is it true that we cannot hear the voice of God?

We *can* hear God's voice. It is the Holy Spirit that tells us about God's will. If we follow the Holy Spirit, He will let us know the will of God.

"But the Counselor, the Holy Spirit, whom the Father will send in my name, will teach you all things and will remind you of everything I have said to you" (Jn. 14:26).

"But when he, the Spirit of truth, comes, he will guide you into all truth. He will not speak on his own; he will speak only what he hears, and he will tell you what is yet to come" (Jn. 16:13).

When we are fully filled with the Holy Spirit, we are able to accomplish God's will. We get to live a life that accomplishes God's plan and purpose. Therefore, we must not forget that the work of Jesus was the work of the Holy Spirit. Jesus wholly followed the Spirit in order to accomplish the will of God for this world (Luke 4:1, Jn. 3:34).

Then, how can we be guided by the Holy Spirit?

When our close friend or relative calls us up, we instantly recognise his or her voice, because we are quite familiar with it. We normally have difficulty in identifying the voices of those whom we meet rarely. Likewise, the Holy Spirit speaks to us with one voice through various channels. Of course, we may get confused because of obstacles, but once we get familiar with the voice of the Holy Spirit, we should be able to easily hear the voice through various channels.

In fact, the Holy Spirit speaks to us in various ways. He uses many channels, but the intent of His word is very clear. Therefore, we sometimes have to interpret the voice by reflecting on its various aspects. We have to comprehensively understand and analyse the voice we have heard through various channels. We may see dangerous results if we only interpret the voice of the Holy Spirit with our dreams, prophecies or visions. Therefore, when we have to make a very important decision, we must have an objective and balanced viewpoint on the voice of the Holy Spirit. Here are some of the methods of getting God's guidance through the Holy Spirit.

The Bible—the voice of God
The Bible is the voice of God, and the Holy Spirit speaks to us through it. The Holy Spirit also speaks to us through dreams, prophecies and visions. But these mystical channels must be interpreted and analysed through the Bible.

Surpassing all boundaries, the Bible clearly shows the will of God regarding all conditions and people. We can learn what God thinks about our various and complex issues. God has already told us about His universal will regarding us through the Bible.

We want to hear something new from God to cope with the problems we face. However, having this desire may amount to disregarding the will of God, which has already been conveyed through the Bible. This is because we want to personally hear something different from God.

The Bible is a book of special revelation. No other book is more special and more unique than the Bible. It is the most fundamental book through which we can hear the voice of God. We can learn about the will and viewpoint of God when we comprehensively study and understand the Bible. Also, we can hear God's voice in full measure when we meditate on the Bible.

Therefore, we should never disregard the Bible. We should pursue the mystical voice that we might hear while we pray. It seems that we have a tendency to disregard God's voice in the Bible and instead consider our own experiences as something special. Wrong religion can result from this approach. If we remain indifferent to the Word of God and seek our own dreams and visions, we may become mystics. Then we would be nothing more than shamans. The only difference would be that we would go to church carrying our Bible in our hand.

The Bible clearly shows us the general and universal will of God. The Ten Commandments is typical of this: "Do not put any other gods in place of me. Remember to keep the Sabbath day holy. Honor your father and mother. Love your neighbor as you love yourself. Do not commit murder. Do not commit adultery. Do not steal. Do not lie."

We have to observe these orders given by God. We have to be faithful in keeping the basic principles. God has clearly ordered us, but we tend to ignore His order and try to personally hear another voice from God instead.

Suppose your mother has dementia. You do your best to serve her. But now you and your wife are worn out and cannot carry on taking care of your mother. What are you going to do about her? You may want to get a special answer from God about it. The Bible says, "Honor your father and mother." God has already told you what to do. You will have to keep your family's condition in mind and use your conscience and wisdom. You will have to choose the best way for your mother and your family. It is God's will for you to find your way through your wisdom and conscience.

However, you may want God to appear in your dream and tell you to send your mother away to an asylum. That is not how God works. Would you take it as the will of God, if he appeared in your dream and told you to abandon your mother on some island far away? Even if God really did tell you to do so in your dream, you would have to give up your dream because it is opposed to the words, "Honor your father and mother." This is a matter of common knowledge and priority. God's word comes before your dream, and we already know the answer through common sense.

The Bible does not always provide solutions to all our problems. It does not say anything about whom we should marry or what kind of job we should have. But God speaks to us when we read the Bible.

We have to read and study the Bible and meditate on it constantly. We will be surprised to find out that the words that we read are so completely fitting to so many of the situations we are in.

"Your word is a lamp to my feet and a light for my path" (Psalms 119:105).

"For the word of God is living and active. Sharper than any double-edged sword, it penetrates even to dividing soul and spirit, joints and marrow; it judges the thoughts and attitudes of the heart" (Hebrews. 4:12).

One day I was reading Deuteronomy chapter 7 with fellow believers. One sister told us about God's voice that she heard while we were meditating on the Word of God. That sister was dating a young man who was not a Christian. She felt that the person she was dating was not the right person in the eyes of God. Her friends also advised her that he was not a suitable match. And while she was reading Deuteronomy chapter 7, verses 2 and 16, words such as "show them no mercy" and "for that will be a snare to you" caught her attention. Then she shared her thoughts with us: "Now I clearly know the will of God. Please pray for me that I could have enough faith in God."

God speaks to us through the Bible. The Holy Spirit gives us valuable insights when we meditate on the Bible. The fact that the same verse can be interpreted according to time and place shows that the Holy Spirit speaks to us through the Word of God.

The Holy Spirit makes the Bible the living Word of God.

Prayer — Interactive channel of communication between man and God

The Holy Spirit speaks to us through our prayer. We cry out to God through our prayer. But this prayer is not a one-sided cry. We can hear what God says to us. Prayer is communication with God. Therefore, it is a big mistake to just talk to God and not to listen to Him.

How does the Holy Spirit speak to us when we pray? It is very likely that the Spirit speaks to us through our mind. Self-assurance grows when the Holy Spirit speaks to us.

When we cannot deeply meet with God through prayer, our thoughts take control of us. And sometimes we mistake our thoughts for the voice of God. I have seen many believers making these kinds of mistakes. There is an unconscious tendency to overlay our thoughts with the voice of God. And we get disappointed when things do not go well. We lose our faith in God.

Experiencing heavenly peace

We have to know that God's voice is different from our thoughts. God gives peace through His voice. But when we mistake our thoughts for God's voice, there is discomfort. It is not comfortable because we made it up to comfort ourselves. The peace that we feel when we hear the voice of the Holy Spirit comes from heaven. It is a mystical peace that we cannot get from this world (John 14:27). Those who have tasted true peace from God would never forget the impression they had.

In the midst of despair we pray, and the Holy Spirit gives us peace. There is no way to explain this heavenly peace. This heavenly peace is like a drug. When you taste it, you see nothing but hope and joy. You would be at peace with yourself, and the people around you may start wondering what keeps you going in life. David experienced this heavenly peace and said, "I will not fear the tens of thousands drawn up against me on every side" (Psalms 6:6).

Being peaceful during troubled times is God's answer. God is implicitly saying that He will solve our problems. I was once worried about my ordination and acquisition of a doctor's degree. But when I prayed in the midst of despair and anxiety, my prayer was answered: I was at peace with myself. The problems that had been plaguing me were solved instantly.

Dreams, visions and prophecies
Joel the prophet prophesied, "I will pour out my Spirit on all people. Your sons and daughters will prophesy, your old men will dream dreams, your young men will see visions" (Joel 2:28).

According to Joel, the Holy Spirit leads us through dreams, visions and prophecies. God works for those who are filled with the Spirit through dreams, visions and prophecies. Of course, God reveals His plan to ordinary people through dreams.

Dreams have special meaning for those who follow the Holy Spirit. Joseph was a dreamer. He was possessed by God's Holy Spirit and God spoke to him through his dreams (Gen. 37:5-11). Through a dream, God told another Joseph, who was going to be the father of Jesus, that Mary had conceived by the Holy Spirit (Mt. 1:18-25). God reveals his plans through our dreams.

When I was a sophomore in seminary I took a test for becoming a chaplain in the army. In my dream, I saw a list of those who had passed the test. But my name was not on the list. I woke up in disappointment to realise that I had actually failed the test. God showed me that becoming a chaplain was not the right course for me.

When I was studying in America, I failed my driving tests twice. On the night before the third test, I saw myself scoring a bullseye and I somehow understood the meaning of that dream. When I easily passed the test and got the license on the following day, I was not much surprised.

Students have to take a general exam before writing a dissertation for a doctor's degree. It takes at least one to two years. God showed me this time as well whether I would pass the exam or not. Life becomes so mysterious when one starts depending on God and following the Holy Spirit.

Again, when I was teaching in a Russian seminary in 1993, I had a dream one October night. In the dream, I saw myself writing a dissertation on Paul Tillich for my doctor's degree and going for gospel preaching. I instantly knew that I would one day do my doctor's course. As I had seen in my dream, I started my doctor's course in 1994 and the title of my dissertation was 'Paul Tillich and Karl Barth's Voiceless Understanding.' Surprisingly, Paul Tillich was a major figure in my dissertation. Thirteen years after having that dream, I realised I had authored four books, namely *Dialogue of Paul Tillich and Karl Barth, Jesus! He Is Coming, Meeting Jesus* and *The Fullness of the Holy Spirit*.

Follow the Holy Spirit and dream of accomplishing world missions and expanding the Church—things that please God.

Cautions for interpreting dreams

However, some cautions must be mentioned:

- Do not force yourself to interpret a dream.
- Do not depend on your dream.
- Drive away evil spirits that work through dreams.

Do not force yourself to interpret a dream
We always want to have a good dream and to interpret it the way we desire. But putting too much effort into interpreting a dream is a waste of labor. We must remember that a dream is a sign from God and that only God can fulfill our dreams. Also, it is not wise to talk about a dream before it is fulfilled.

Do not depend on your dream
Dreams cannot control us. Only God has control over us. Dreams are just one of God's methods of revealing His plan to us. Whether you dream or not, the will of God will be done. If you have a good dream, wait for it to be fulfilled. When the dream is fulfilled, thank God for it, for it was He who gave you that dream. Pray to God if you have a bad dream.

Drive away evil spirits that work through dreams
Sometimes evil spirits bother us through our dreams. Ignore them. Those who believe in Jesus need not fear dreams. Tell the evil spirits that trouble you in your dream to go away in the name of Jesus Christ. Some people get bound to their bad dreams. They forget that a dream is just a dream. It may or may not come true.

God shows the way through visions
I was a junior at Seoul Theological University in 1989 and preparing for the admission exam for Yonsei Seminary to study theology further. One day, in December, a sister whom I was dating said, "I was praying for you and I saw a big pencil."

I wondered what that 'big pencil' meant. So I seriously talked about it with her. She was also studying theology and was known for praying for more than an hour in one place. God had given her the gift of seeing visions.

This 'big pencil' pointed at the idea of studying abroad. During those days many students went either to Germany or America to study theology. I preferred America because I had been studying English for quite some time. So we concluded that the meaning of the 'big pencil' was my going to America to study. I changed my direction from Yonsei Seminary to America. Some people might laugh at me and say, "What a pity! You changed your future after seeing a *pencil* in your vision!"

However, her prophecy turned out to be true. After I made up my mind to go to America to study, I began to experience many miracles. One of them was improvement in my health. I was physically weak and could not study for long at a stretch. I had to take herbal medicines several times. But since the time I decided to go to America, a strange power started to spring up inside me. In the winter of the same year I was staying in the school dormitory to prepare for going abroad. No sooner had I started taking a cold shower than I realised that the water did not feel unbearably cold! Something had happened to me. So I called my father and said, "Dad! Something had happened to me. I took a cold shower a little while ago, but I am not cold."

Another miracle came in the form of my TOEFL score. I had only four months to study for the test because my going to America was based on a sudden decision. However, in April 1990, I got a score that was enough to apply for graduate school in America. And it was the first TOEFL test I had ever taken. Usually, one prepares for the TOEFL test for quite a long time. Truly, it was God who had helped me. God had not only helped me to do well in the test, but had also helped me to have good concentration during the four months of preparation time.

Besides, I got an 'A' for the first semester in my senior year. In fact, my school grades were very poor. I did study hard but grades did not come out that well. I studied harder after I made up my mind to go to America but all 'A' was like a dream to me. The important thing was that one of the major conditions for admission was good school grades.

More miracles happened. On September 29, 1990, I married the sister who had seen the 'big pencil' in her vision. I was 23 years old and a senior student. I hurried my wedding because Dr. Conklin, who was a visiting professor to Seoul Theological University, had advised me to do so. She was a professor of social psychology at Houghton College in America. Dr. Conklin said it would be better to get married before I went to America to study, as we, a newly-wed couple, may find it difficult to adapt to new conditions and a new place.

I strongly believed that God would send me to America. So I prepared for my wedding. But our families did not have enough money, nor were they ready for our marriage. Once again God helped us: My relatives provided us with $1,200 and our marriage took place in the best possible manner.

We had yet another problem to resolve. We did not have a place to live. My aunt was kind enough to let us stay in her house.

Many of those whom -I knew were critical of my marriage. One of my seniors said, "You should have been more responsible!" I was speechless.

I received a letter of admission to school from Drew University in America on December 26, 1990. Next, I gave a visa interview and got the visa. Finally, I entered Drew University. I had to miss my graduation ceremony in Korea.

I left for America on January 16, 1991. It was God who made my studying in America possible. A miracle had happened!

The Holy Spirit speaks to us through various gifts. However, compared to the Word of God and prayer, dreams, visions and prophecy are just assisting methods. We must realise that the Holy Spirit has already spoken to us through the Bible, and therefore we should regularly read the Bible and carefully listen to the voice of God. The Holy Spirit also speaks to us through prayer. The presence of mystical peace during or after prayer is the voice of Holy Spirit.

If we choose something that God does not want, peace from the Holy Spirit leaves and fear and instability given by evil spirits come. But when we choose what God wants us to choose, fear leaves us and peace comes to us. Maybe peace is the voice of the Holy Spirit and fear and instability are the voices of evil spirits.

We can clearly hear the voice of the Holy Spirit through the Bible and prayer. Therefore it is not right for believers to hold onto only dreams, visions and prophecy. Do not force yourself to hear the voice of the Holy Spirit through dreams, visions and prophecy. Accept them naturally. Some people get nervous if they do not see dreams or visions. I also worried that I would become that kind of person. We must give more importance to God's words than to mystical gifts. Therefore, we should study the Bible regularly.

Circumstances — the last sign of the Holy Spirit

Through prayer, the Word of God, dreams, visions and prophecy the voice of the Holy Spirit is heard. If God's promise, which is spoken through the Holy Spirit, is not kept, we should say that the voice of the Holy Spirit is just a myth. We may have heard the wrong voice or mistaken our own voice for the voice of the Holy Spirit. Another possibility is that the time may not be ripe for the promise to be kept. So, we should wait.

We should overcome our problems through faith. But if our prayers are not answered quickly, we must conclude that God does not want things to change in our lives. In such a situation, we must patiently wait and earnestly pray to God.

To Gideon, the judge in the Old Testament age, an angel of the Lord came. The angel told him that he would save Israel and that God would be with him to win over the Midian army. Gideon wanted to make sure that what he had heard from God would come true. He wanted to confirm that the voice of God and the situation in which he was matched each other. He worried that he might do something wrong obsessed by something other than God. So he asked God twice to give him proofs (Judges 6:36-40).

First, he asked God to wet the fleece of wool with dew and let the ground stay dry. Then he asked again to wet the ground and let the fleece of wool remain dry. Perhaps, Gideon's faith may seem like the doubtful faith of Thomas. But through his story we can learn that God's promise is kept in the situation in which we happen to be.

During my study in America I applied twice for permanent residency. I wanted to get the residency for my children, who had American citizenship. I definitely needed it because there were various benefits that accompanied it, such as bank loans, social welfare and getting a job easily. I thought there was no reason that God should not give me the residency. So my wife and I prayed hard when we worshipped at home.

However, we failed to get it. The first reason was that our application was not moving. I thought it was because I had engaged an ordinary lawyer. I used an African American woman lawyer but it seemed that she was not taking care of the documents. She just kept us waiting and waiting. So after a year, I cancelled the contract. Two years later, I engaged an efficient lawyer. The lawyer was Korean-American, and it took less than a year to get the application passed. I was relieved after signing the contract with him. I was confident that God would let me to have the residency. But something rather unexpected happened. Another person, who did not have a good condition, received the residency and mine was withheld.

Finally, the Immigration and Naturalization Service (INS) told me to submit supplementary documents. My lawyer said that it would take a year to hand in those documents. So I had to give up. I was really hurt and I complained to God, "I did my best and tried hard to get this residency, God. It seems you don't want me to have it." Now, I know that I wrong. I was not listening to God's voice. If I had received the residency, I would not have been what I am now. We must never disregard the voice of the Holy Spirit—even when we cannot see a way out of the situation in which we are and feel that our prayers have not been answered, Jacob worked for 20 years for his uncle Laban. He became his son-in-law by marrying his daughters. When Jacob became very rich, Laban, his uncle and his father-in-law, started to feel uncomfortable (Gen. 31:1-2). Perhaps Jacob wanted to get more animals from Laban. He may have wanted to go back to his father and mother; but he also wanted to stay a little longer, because he wanted to possess Laban's animals.

Now Laban and his sons' attitude toward Jacob had changed. Then God told Jacob to go back to his homeland (Gen. 31:3). Maybe God had already told him many times to go back. But Jacob might have ignored His voice or could not even have heard it. Jacob might have finally heard God's voice after seeing a rather uncomfortable relationship develop between him and his uncle.

I worked at a Russian seminary from 1993 to 1994. American, Russian and Korean professors taught at that school. I taught theology and was in charge of the school administration. Students looked up to me, and professors and deans looked for my help. I also wanted to devote myself to Russian ministry, but God did not let me. I was regarded as a foreign student so I had to take a doctoral course in America in order to get my passport extended. Another way was to continue my ministry by getting an American green card.

God did not allow my passport extension. A letter came from a university in America telling me that they would cancel my admission unless I started my doctoral course there. So I had to stop my ministry in Russia and go back to America to start the doctoral course. I realised that no matter how much I wanted to work for God, I had to do what God actually wanted me to do. We must remember that in our attempt to please God by doing what we are doing, we sometimes end up displeasing Him.

Father of three children joins the army
My doctoral course in America started again in 1994. When I finished my course my passport expired. I had to go back to Korea and be enlisted in the army. But I had faith that I would be exempted and continue my study. I felt it a burden to be enlisted at a rather old age, and moreover, I really wanted to get a doctoral degree. Also, I was a father of three children.

According to the Korean Military Manpower Administration, military service could be exempted if one had two family members to support. I had three children, so I never imagined that I would be enlisted.

However, God wanted me to join the army. He wanted me to go to the front-line area facing North Korea. This is the story of my enlistment. I had to join the army because the support rate of two family members could be applied to different conditions. My mother died during that time and my father remarried. My step-mother's age was less, which meant that she was not a subject of support. According to the law, her age was enough to work to support family members. This meant that my mother could support two of my children, which left me with only one to support.

Another condition for exemption was the age of my father. If he was 60 years old, he could be a subject of support, which satisfied two members for me. But he was 59 years and 2 months old. 10 months less than 60. There was yet another condition. I myself could be a subject of support if I get a 'public service' rate in the physical examination. There were also other conditions to get exempted from military service. But God did not let those conditions block my way.

Eventually and miraculously, I became a Private First Class of the Korean Army. I would be the first and the last person recorded on the military data as one who had three children, except for the time of the Korean War. My army life was terrible. I could not freely enjoy my religious life. I experienced nothing but pain and frustration. Why did God send me to the army? I could not understand God's ways. There were three colleagues who went to America to study theology. They all got US citizenship and were all exempted from military service. I was the only one who joined the army. I wondered why God had pushed me to be in such an odd situation.

"God, wouldn't it be better for me to finish my doctoral course? Don't you think it is a waste of time to be stuck deep inside a mountain? Why did you put me in this desolate place and not let me study?"

God answered my questions after I completed my military service. I started to thank God for sending me to the army.

Although it was quite late, I agreed with God's plan and intent and I thanked Him for it.

God speaks to us through our environment. I experienced God's silence about my sufferings when I was in the army. I was really disappointed with God. If he was so determined to send me to the army, he could have sent me to a place where I could use English or somewhere where I could work easily. But he sent me to the toughest mountain area with the worst transportation in Korea. It was so tough that they had even composed a song on it, "Oh, how can I return with this grief and so much concern!" To make things worse, God sent me to an artillery battalion, one of the toughest units in the Korean army.

I was a chaplain solider in my first year. My duty was to help other soldiers maintain their religious and mental health. But my chaplain work was tough. My company leader was three years younger than me and he was a theology major at Yonsei University. The chaplain, who was a pastor, was my age. And my senior soldier was a student majoring in theology. There were three people who majored in theology around me. It was obvious that they did not like me—someone who had studied theology in America.

Also, I had a problem. It was difficult for me to have a modest attitude towards all of them. God wanted to break me down. I experienced God in silence. God had put me in a situation where I was helpless. However, his silence was the answer. He was telling me to get lower than ever and to change. I found myself searching for the mystical voice and saving hand of God instead of trying to understand the voice of the Holy Spirit.

Finally, I had to stop working as a chaplain and I had to work as a normal battalion soldier. There I experienced another bout of God's silence. I could not pray whenever I was on sentry at night. My soul was in despair. When I was on duty in daylight I gazed upon a flowing river beside a sentry post. The river was flowing, but time was static.

My heart was heavy and I found army life rather tough. I had to prepare for battalion evaluation conducted by our higher command although I had never handled any artillery in over a year. This training was called battalion ATT. It was conducted every three years and it was the toughest training. I had no knowledge of artillery and I became a chief senior soldier who had to take responsibility for the artillery in conducting battalion ATT.

I received training to death. I actually shot 21 live artillery shells during the training and evaluation. Most of the artillery soldiers rarely shoot even one live shell before completing their service. But I shot many shells. And my battalion won the first place in that evaluation. Without knowing it, I was not a chaplain soldier anymore. I became a ferocious senior soldier who scolded and swore at juniors.

The tough army life I led gave me valuable insights into my limitations. I learned that I was selfish, dirty, incapable and weak. God was kind to me, but He remained silent during my army life. Later on, I realised that His silence was actually the voice of the Holy Spirit. For this reason, the words of Paul in Romans, which describe humans very negatively, sprung up deep inside my heart (Romans 1:28-32, 3:10-18).

Chapter 2
In the midst of strains of faith and environment

People who believe in Jesus should not fear their environment. With faith in God, they can make rivers in desert. There is nothing that the Almighty God cannot do. However, God sometimes remains silent. Sometimes He just lets us be where we happen to be and reveals His will through our environment.

Unyielding faith can change the environment, but that faith may have originated from us, not from God. The moment we practice this kind of faith, we see the tension between our unyielding faith and the environment. We cannot tell exactly what the will of God is because it varies according to situation and time. This is why we should not let go of anything. Remember that Jericho, which seemed impossible to take down, collapsed so easily when the Israelites were praying and that Ai, which was so small and weak, made the Israelites despair.

Therefore we should never lose faith in God and keep trying until we succeed. We must not be disappointed when our faith does not work. Instead, we must try to carefully listen to the voice of the Holy Spirit. Many Christians ignore the environment or the obstacles they face by completely depending on their faith. They do not make a determined effort to solve their problems. In contrast, non-believers, who do not depend on God's power, try hard to perfect their work. We must try to strike a balance between these two approaches or "voices."

We may find it difficult to discern the voice of the Holy Spirit when confronted with these two voices. To overcome this difficulty, all we need to do is strengthen our relationship with God. Avoid drawing hasty conclusions. Try to be patient and always walk with the Holy Spirit.

God has different time tables

Sometimes we miss our target by a narrow margin. Then we learn that it was not God's plan for us to achieve our immediate goal. Sometimes we find ourselves stuck in difficult situations and we do not know how to get out of them. We are caught in His time.

God controls our environment and time through His will. In His time, we sometimes experience highly significant events (Ecc. 9:11-12).

I remember that I wrote a letter to Reverend P who was ministering in Chicago right before I finished my dissertation. I asked him to introduce me to a church where I could minister as a senior pastor. Reverend P was kind to other people and he had a gift from God to introduce his junior pastors to churches. I did not want to go back to Korea. I longed to minister at a Korean church and wanted my children to learn more English instead. But there was no answer from him and I finished my dissertation.

So my family of five had to come back to Korea. We moved into my parents' small house with six pieces of baggage. Winter had finally set in, so we wore heavy clothes and hung them on hangers. The small house was full of people and thermal wear. And then I had to start a so-called 'peddler's life' in Korea. I got approval to teach a class at Seoul Theological Seminary, where I graduated. Also, I got one class each at Soongsil University and Hoseo University. One day I received an e-mail message from Reverend P. It said that he had tried to find me for one month after he got a church to introduce to me. It was after I had come back to Korea and searched for a job. I really wanted to go back to America, begging for forgiveness to the schools where I was supposed to teach. However, something that I cannot tell for sure did not allow me to go. I regard it as the voice of the Holy Spirit. I was destined to work in Korea according to His time. I mumbled to myself: "Why is God so against my wish to live in America? Why can't I get residency and why can't I minister in America?"

But I clearly knew that it was the will of God. I heard the voice of God through my environment and time. The voice of the Holy Spirit told me that I had to work for God in Korea.

Harmonising common sense with mystery

"He chose capable men from all Israel and made them leaders of the people, officials over thousands, hundreds, fifties and tens. They served as judges for the people at all times. The difficult cases they brought to Moses, but the simple ones they decided themselves" (Ex. 18:25-26).

There were too many Israelites, and Moses just could not manage them all by himself. So he appointed leaders of thousands, hundreds, fifties, and tens to take care of 'easy cases.' Moses himself took care of 'difficult cases.'

From this passage we learn that there are easy things and difficult things. Easy things may refer to general and common things and difficult things to something that is spiritual and divine.

Non-believers use their common sense in all of their work. They deny things that cannot be understood with their reason and rationality. They do not value religion or mystery or spiritual faith. On the other hand, believers take the spiritual side to manage their work. They desire to pursue the mysterious and spiritual world, which surpasses common sense and reality. Here we see that non-believers and believers have very different attitudes towards life.

Perhaps common sense and mystery run in parallel lines. Can we really harmonise them? I think that what Moses did was based on his pursuit of harmonising common sense with mystery. It is difficult to blend those two. But for those who have good faith, all they have to do is to add common sense.

Many believers run into problems because they completely ignore common sense. They only try to listen to what God is saying through dreams and visions. They do not try to use the common sense that God has given to them. Also, some believers have a problem because they are too smart. I do not really like believers who have no faith but talk only about common knowledge and ungodly stories. But it is so heartbreaking to see people with good faith suffering hardships because they have ignored common sense.

Often there are believers in church who cause problems because they only pursue mystery. We are human beings. We need common sense and human relationships. Think about God who became a human. He had to become a human being because he felt too heavy! We need to have knowledge of science, ethics, society, culture and other fields. Mystical faith is required upon this worldly foundation.

God sometimes uses human ways
We often ask God to do things that we have to do. We pray to God to help us get good grades in school, but we do not

put forth efforts to study. We ask Him to send us a good spouse, but we say 'no' to someone who wishes to introduce a 'future-spouse.' Again, a man prays to God for a new place. So he puts out his house for sale. People come to see his house, but they find it small and unclean. This man keeps praying to God for the right buyer to appear.

Had I been in such a situation and had I received the answer from God, I would have cleaned up my house, painted the walls and removed useless furniture. God wants us to use common sense in doing things that we have to do ourselves. God is spirit and so He wishes to work through humans. But it is foolish to put God aside and to work using only human methods. At the same time, it is not wise to be careless about the 'things we have to do' while saying 'I believe in God almighty.' It is always graceful when mystery and common sense are combined.

Spiritual issues are more important than human issues. Spiritual mysteries are more valuable than common sense. However, there is a strong working of the Holy Spirit when common sense and human issues are backing up the mystery. If spiritual and mysterious things do not have any relationship with common knowledge and human methods, it would be just like stepping on the accelerator of a car without putting it in gear. It is nothing more than idling.

Suppose there is a pastor who is good at preaching and prays a lot. Every Sunday morning people come to him and are greatly moved by his words. But if this pastor does not visit his people often and is too busy to meet them, believers would turn their backs on him. It is quite obvious, because he has no regard for his church members.

Now consider another pastor. He is a poor preacher and does not really pray much. But he regularly visits his people.

He invites them to dinner and comforts them when they have difficulties. Church members like him more for his kindness than for his spirituality.

Nevertheless, God does not support the pastor who only insists on building human relationships. No matter how often he invites people to his house for dinner and how many gifts he gives out, his efforts would prove to be useless if he fails to please God.

When the principle of the cross is well established, the will of God can be delivered at its utmost, and the most powerful work of the Holy Spirit can be experienced. The vertical relationship with God and the horizontal relationship with the world have to be harmonised. But the vertical relationship with God should come first, not the horizontal relationship with the world. A pastor who is a good preacher and fervently prays to God with much love for his church members, whom he visits regularly and cares for, is the ideal pastor.

Disregarding common sense leads to blind spirituality
Big problems will occur if you disregard your environment and only pursue vertical spirituality. Jesus told us to be harmless as doves and wise as snakes. The wisdom Jesus spoke of here could be the wisdom of applying well our common sense to our spirituality. Truly, we need the holistic discernment that enables us to distinguish between things to approach spiritually and things to approach with common sense. The Holy Spirit is the spirit that transcends everything, but He is also the spirit who lives in our flesh and blood.

Today's world requires holistic spirituality with the transcendence and immanence of the Holy Spirit, common sense and mystery and superb harmonisation of spirit and body. The Holy Spirit does not show up only in our dreams and visions. He also comes to us through common sense and knowledge. All we need to do is strike a balance between mystical spirituality and common sense.

Importance of psychological treatment

People of prayer might disregard psychology. As often as not, Christian parents, who rely only on their faith, get exhausted while raising their children. Why does this happen? It is because Christian parents ignore common sense. They must fulfill the psychological, mental and physical needs of their children in accordance with the age of the children. There are several things that parents must do for their children.

Faith can be developed with just an ice cream for some children. Good listening can also bring about a change in the attitude of children. A little bit of discipline can also have a positive effect on them. All of these are psychological treatments.

However, many believers do not give importance to psychological treatment. They say prayer is more than enough. Of course, God does listen to their prayer, but the prayer may not be answered immediately. If you fulfill your child's psychological and mental needs while praying to God, you will see marvelous changes in your child.

Nowadays children are becoming idols of their parents. How can parents force their children to have religion when their children have already become their idols? This is the problem of the modern Korean church. Believers seem to have strong faith, but actually their god is their children. However, satisfying the emotional and psychological needs of children is another problem. Some parents expect too much from their children, while other parents just let their children do whatever they want to without temperance. They raise their children with loose love. What is the will of God for our children?

God's will is to teach our children how to establish their relationship with God, not by force but by proper guidance. If we are aware of our children's psychology, we will find it easier to help them to build up their faith. Good faith and a deep understanding of your children's psychology will surely make you an ideal parent. That is why we as parents should read good books on child psychology. The Holy Spirit also speaks through books—a point that most Korean Christian parents fail to understand.

God speaks through people's advice
The Holy Spirit speaks to us through people as well. Now, we hear so many voices every day. Therefore, we must be spiritually sharp enough to identify the voice of the Holy Spirit.

Jethro, who was Moses' father-in-law, saw Moses leading and judging millions of people all by himself. So he gave Moses his insightful advice. Jethro thought that it was not wise to do the work all by himself. So he told Moses to appoint leaders of thousands, hundreds and fifties and have them do the easy work. This was really a magnificent idea that came down from heaven. Through whom did it come? It was through Jethro, Moses' father-in-law. Who was Jethro? He was not Hebrew. He was a foreigner!

The Holy Spirit can speak to us through anybody. So we should always keep our spiritual ears open. God spoke through a donkey as well. Jesus said the stones will cry out if people keep quiet. God is spirit and therefore He can use anything to speak to us. He can use voiceless things, such as trees, stones, mountains and seas, to speak to us. He can also use animals that can make sounds—such as birds, donkeys, cows and dogs. We can hear God's voice through the Bible and while we are praying, but the Holy Spirit also speaks to us through various people to clarify Himself.

However, the Holy Spirit does not always speak to us through the same person. To make things worse, evil spirits also speak to us through different people. Thus, in order to correctly identify the voice of the Holy Spirit, we must maintain a strong relationship with the Holy Spirit.

A test I did not want to take

I received my Master's degree in May 1993. After that I had to take the TOEFL test in order to enroll for a doctoral course. During that time, the master's course required a score of 550, and 600 was required for a doctoral course. I was a graduate of a master's course, but it was not easy for me to improve my TOEFL score. TOEFL was absolutely irrelevant to my school study. I had to focus only on the test to raise my score. I took the test twice in America but my score was not good enough. I could not go to a TOEFL tutoring school, which I would have done if I were in Korea. I really did not know what to do because 'no TOEFL score' meant 'no doctoral course.'

Then came my daughter's first birthday party. I celebrated her birthday with my friends at the seminary. I was exhausted after the party. On the following day, I had to take the test. I gave up that night, as I was too tired and was not ready. It was obvious that I would fail the test because I had not studied even for an hour! Also, the test centre was in Jersey City, a black neighborhood in New Jersey where I had never been before.

The next morning at 7 o'clock, the phone rang. It was pastor S from a Presbyterian church. He called me because he knew that I was taking the test on that day. Pastor S asked me to accompany him because he did not know Jersey City well. He was also supposed to take the test on that day. I was tired and I was not confident of getting a good score so I refused. But when pastor S begged me to go with him I yielded. Pastor S drove and I held a map to help him find the way.

When I received the test paper, something really strange happened. While taking the vocabulary test I realised, much to my amazement, that I knew all of the answers. So I scored well on the vocabulary test. Also, the test supervisor during the comprehension test was really generous. It was difficult for students to take the test because of stringent regulations. But that day the supervisor made the students feel at ease. After the test, I met pastor S and exchanged answers. At that moment I knew that I would get a good score. I kept on saying, "Thank you God!"

When I longed for a good score, I failed the test. But when I wanted to drop the whole idea of taking the test, the Holy Spirit sent pastor S to tell me to take the test.

Look for expert advice!
The Holy Spirit speaks to us through people. This is why we should seek people's advice before making important decisions. We should seek advice especially from experts. We cannot say their advice is from the Holy Spirit, but the Holy Spirit uses knowledge gained by experts.

We normally talk to a real-estate expert if we plan to move to a new place. We talk to an architect and a designer if we plan to build a house. We call a lawyer to discuss legal issues. We can also become experts after interacting with experts for some time. That is when the Holy Spirit uses the knowledge that we gained. If you have heard God's voice while reading the Bible or while praying, then you can bring forth a good piece of work with the vision you received from the Holy Spirit together with your expertise and effort.

It would be really foolish to ignore the advice of experts or experienced people and to just hold on to our dream or vision in carrying out our work. Know that God's work always works together with our environment.

We ask the Holy Spirit to show a new place for our home or church through our dreams. Sometimes the Holy Spirit does show something in our dreams. But He does not do that for all believers. This is why we have to carefully listen to Him. Remember that the Holy Spirit uses architects, designers, real-estate experts, etc., around us. Their expertise can help us when we are on our knees and praying to God. But this expertise can hinder God's will to those who do not have faith.

We need to consult experts about issues related to children's education, marriage, and so on. Their approach may not be religious. But the Holy Spirit uses worldly knowledge. We can get the best result when we add worldly and expert knowledge to our faith, just like Moses, who effectively administered the Israelites by taking Jethro's advice.

Walk with the Holy Spirit
To follow the voice and guidance of the Holy Spirit:

- *Do not draw a hasty conclusion about God's will*

    "An inheritance quickly gained at the beginning will not be blessed at the end" (Prov. 20:21). Decisions made in haste only produce bad outcomes. We should follow the example of Gideon, one of the judges of the Old Testament. Have enough time to calmly think about and to discern the will of God. By doing so, you will not make any mistakes while obeying the Holy Spirit.

- *Interpret comprehensively*

    To discern the voice of the Holy Spirit, we should first refer to the Bible. Look at the work to see whether it is based on the Bible or not. Give enough time for prayer and search for peace given by the Spirit. As a supplement, we may refer to the voice of the Holy Spirit spoken through dreams, visions, or prophecies. To avoid any possibilities of inclination to heresy or mysticism, maintain practical observation and analysis.

- *Wait for the final proof from the environment*

    When David and Bathsheba's first child was dying, David fasted and cried out to God to save his child. But God did not let the child live. As soon as his child died, David stopped his fasting and ate. David's servants were puzzled by his sudden change of attitude. David said to his servants, "While the child was alive, I fasted and wept; for I said, 'Who can tell whether the LORD will be gracious to me, that the child may live?' But now that he is dead, why should I fast? Can I bring him back again? I will go to him, but he will not return to me" (2Sam. 12:22-23). God is the one who has the final authority and He speaks to us through our environment. It may seem an act of faith to insist that something is the Will of God, when in fact it may not be true. Our conclusion may be based on our personal belief. We must never mistake our belief for the voice of the Holy Spirit.

- *Keep a balance between faith and environment, mystery and common sense*

    If you have a "rational and critical" faith, you should stop focusing too much on your environment and common sense. If you do not ask for the mysterious work of the Holy Spirit, your faith will dry up and you will make the Holy Spirit sad. If your faith is "fervent and emotional," you should start focusing on your environment and common sense. You must give a lot of importance to listening to the voice of the Holy Spirit while praying and to having dreams and visions. But you must not denounce the idea of seeking advice and guidance from experts as a waste of time. Maintain a balance between mystery and common sense and the Holy Spirit will always be there to help you.

Chapter 3

What does the Holy Spirit do?

Christianity as a religion holds great mysteries. How can Christians possibly worship a young man named Jesus as God? Why do we have to believe in Jesus? Can God really become a human? Why should we bother about things that happened 2,000 years ago in Israel? More often than not, our rational mind compels us to regard Christianity as a figment of imagination. Many non-believers regard the story of virgin birth and resurrection of Jesus as a myth.

However, it is interesting to see that there are so many people who believe in Jesus and consider Him as the Son of God. For the last 2,000 years Christianity has been the state religion of Rome and the most influential religion in the world. According to a CNN broadcast, Jesus Christ is the most influential person in the world—someone who influenced the history of the world for over 2,000 years.

How could this be? It is truly mysterious and marvelous. How could people regard Jesus as the Son of God? How could people give their lives for Jesus? The Holy Spirit is the answer to these questions. The Holy Spirit enables people to believe in Jesus.

When a person is possessed by the Holy Spirit, he starts acting strangely. He or she may be scientific and rational, but once possessed by the Holy Spirit, he or she will begin to regard Jesus as the Son of God and believe in non-scientific and irrational events such as virgin birth and resurrection of Jesus. Paul said, "No one can say 'Jesus is Lord,' except by the Holy Spirit" (2 Cor. 12:3).

The Holy Spirit is not a superhuman being or some kind of energy. He is a personal being who comes and sees each and every one of us. "God is spirit, and his worshipers must worship in spirit and in truth" (Jn. 4:24). That is why people completely change when the Holy Spirit comes into them. Just like the word of God, "Not by might nor by power, but by my Spirit" (Zec. 4:6), non-believers go crazy in a good way when they are possessed by the Holy Spirit; they are born again (Jn 3:5-8).

The Holy Spirit is God. The Bible says that the Father, the Son and the Holy Spirit are the LORD. That is why Matthew 28:19 says, "Therefore go and make disciples of all nations, baptizing them in the name of the Father and of the Son and of the Holy Spirit." Also, Paul gave his blessing by saying, "May the grace of the Lord Jesus Christ, and the love of God, and the fellowship of the Holy Spirit be with you all" (2 Cor. 13:13).

The Holy Spirit is the Triune God. As Jesus was ascending to Heaven he sent another Counselor, the Holy Spirit. Through the Holy Spirit we feel the presence of Jesus. This is because Jesus is always present within the Holy Spirit. The Bible says that the Holy Spirit is the Spirit of Christ.

General ministry: Creation and preservation
Together with the Father and the Son, the Holy Spirit created the universe and until today he has been taking care of this world with His providence (Gen. 1:1-2). The creation and preservation of the world is the general ministry of the Holy Spirit and at the same time it is the joint ministry of the Father

and the Son. "The LORD God formed the man from the dust of the ground and breathed into his nostrils the breath of life, and the man became a living being" (Gen. 2:7). It is the Holy Spirit that derived the creation and by which the universe is being maintained. The Holy Spirit works within this world. It is the strength of the life of God.

Special ministry: Completion of salvation

In addition to the Holy Spirit's general ministry, there is a special ministry that only belongs to the Holy Spirit. It is the completion of salvation. The Holy Spirit convicts the world in regard to sin, witnesses to Jesus and saves sinners (Jn. 16:7-11). The Holy Spirit works to apply the objective event of salvation that took place 2,000 years ago to our present lives. The Holy Spirit makes us believe in Jesus and completes the saving ministry of Jesus Christ.

The Holy Spirit enabled the ministry of Jesus on earth

Believers in the first century regarded Jesus of Nazareth as Christ (the anointed one, the messiah). They believed that Jesus was the Christ that the prophets of the Old Testament had been talking about and that He was especially filled with the Holy Spirit to the fullest. The birth of Jesus was very unusual. It was the work of the Holy Spirit. Gabriel the angel proclaimed to Mary, "The Holy Spirit will come upon you, and the power of the Most High will overshadow you." The Holy Spirit endowed Jesus with the ability to heal and to drive out evil spirits. Jesus conquered the grave and was resurrected through the power of the Holy Spirit. Jesus' ministry on earth was indeed full of the Holy Spirit.

The Holy Spirit inspired the writers of the Bible

The Bible is the book of salvation (2 Tim. 3:15). It is the only book that testifies to the saving ministry of Jesus Christ. We meet Jesus through the Bible. However, in the absence of the Holy Spirit we may not be able to say that Jesus is God and that all the other miracles mentioned in the Bible are true. Because the Bible was written under the inspiration of the Holy Spirit, it would not be wrong to regard the Holy Spirit as the original writer of the Bible (2 Tim. 3:16-17).

The Holy Spirit makes believers to be born again

We are born again when we truly start believing in Jesus. Only the Holy Spirit can make this possible because when the Spirit is within us, He makes us realise that we are sinners and that Jesus shed his blood for our sins.

The Holy Spirit is the builder of the Church

The Holy Spirit descended upon the people at Pentecost and opened a new age, the age of church mission. Jesus proclaimed to his disciples (who were trembling with fear) that the Holy Spirit would come. What Jesus had said happened at Pentecost. The descent of the Holy Spirit on that day was a historical and objective event (Acts 2:1-4). "But you will receive power when the Holy Spirit comes on you; and you will be my witnesses in Jerusalem, and in all Judea and Samaria, and to the ends of the earth" (Acts 1:8). Jesus' disciples received the Holy Spirit and, starting from Jerusalem, they witnessed the Gospel of Jesus through Rome and throughout the world. They became a truly powerful people and the world was not worthy of them. The eleven apostles who received the Holy Spirit and preached the Gospel were martyred. Upon their death, the church was planted in this world.

The Holy Spirit makes believers have an intimate relationship with God

The Holy Spirit gives us the conviction that we are the children of God (Jn. 1:12). And He helps believers to maintain a close relationship with God. The Holy Spirit not only helps us to come to God, but also helps us in our prayer (Rm. 8:26). He makes us to be strongly held by God. We hear God's voice when we pray in the Spirit. And we can enjoy the blessings of God when we obey His voice.

What is the best gift we can get from God? Perhaps, it is the Holy Spirit, the Counselor. This is true because only the Holy Spirit can help us to firmly believe in Jesus. When we maintain steadfast faith in Jesus through the help of the Holy Spirit, God showers His blessings on us. This is why we should always seek the Holy Spirit.

"If you then, though you are evil, know how to give good gifts to your children, how much more will your Father in heaven give the Holy Spirit to those who ask him!" (Lk. 11:13).

Going to church, giving offerings and being a nice person are not enough. These are just religious activities that lack life and vitality. Our faith will be like an empty shell if we do not have the Spirit. Any great believer can become a castaway if the Holy Spirit leaves him or her. King Saul and Samson are good examples of such people. King David knew the secret of the Holy Spirit. So he prayed to God when he sinned against God, "Do not take your Holy Spirit from me!" David did not mind if God took away everything he had, but he just could not afford to lose the Holy Spirit.

We need to have the Holy Spirit within us. The presence of the Holy Spirit is the key to receiving God's blessings. It is also the secret of having firm faith in Jesus Christ. We have to follow the Holy Spirit. We need to please the Holy Spirit. In order to do that, we should be wise enough to choose the things that please the Holy Spirit. For this we need to have spiritual discernment and almost complete knowledge of the Holy Spirit.

Chapter 4
How can we tell we are filled with the Holy Spirit?

When we receive the Holy Spirit, we repent of our past sins and accept Jesus as our savior. The Holy Spirit does not forsake believers (2 Co. 3:16). Most of us feel that the Holy Spirit stays with us as long as our faith is strong. This is not true. The Holy Spirit leaves us only when we give up our faith and deny Jesus Christ (Jn. 14:16-17).

Paul urged us to be in the fullness of the Holy Spirit. He also asked us not to grieve the Holy Spirit (Eph. 4:30). When we disobey God and fall into temptations of sin, the Holy Spirit grieves and takes back His presence and power. But when we repent and ask for the fullness of the Spirit, He comes back and works with His powers.

The Holy Spirit comes like a strong and fast wind
We can learn something about the Holy Spirit through Acts 2:2. It depicts the presence of the Holy Spirit as a strong and fast wind. In this regard, being in the fullness of the Holy Spirit may sometimes shake our body like a leaf being blown in the wind. In my church, there was a deaconess named Mrs. Son who prayed much. I observed her praying. She usually prayed gently, but when the Holy Spirit came with

strong presence, she started to jerk. The stronger the presence of the Holy Spirit, the stronger and more pleasantly she prayed. After the prayer, her eyes shone with excitement and joy. My heart overflowed with joy whenever I saw her shaking while praying in the presence of the Holy Spirit. Our church had a prayer meeting every night from 10:00 pm to 1:00 or 2:00 am. Recently a deaconess received the Holy Spirit to the fullest. Church members laid hands on her and asked God to give her tongues. As an answer to our prayer, the Holy Spirit came to her in strong presence. She was a woman of a small figure with a feeble voice, but when the Holy Spirit came, she burst out with tongues with a forceful voice. She also began to jerk all over and started to roll her neck, which caused a lot of distraction. She rolled her neck, jerked up and down and fell to the floor. Then she got up, continued to pray and then she fell down again. Through her experience I learned that in the presence of the Holy Spirit, there can be a strong jerking that the body cannot bear.

The scene she made was something really new to me. It was so unusual and strange. So I just watched all her bodily movements. After the prayer meeting we talked about it. She said that her body vibrated because the power of the Holy Spirit was so strong and that she could not restrain from rotating her neck and fell down because she felt so dizzy. Mrs. Son told us that she too had the same experience and said, "You can control the jerking." From that day on, the deaconess started to control the rotating of her neck. She stopped falling down because of dizziness, and her prayer became more powerful. Through her experience, I, who was a pastor, newly learned that my body could also be strongly shaken when the Holy Spirit came like a wind and that when it seemed that I could not do anything about the jerking, actually I could control it with my mind.

She began to jerk her body and roll her neck while she was fervently praying. That night, our prayer meeting was strongly driven by the Holy Spirit. But the deaconess vomited when she got back home and suffered sharp pains all over her body. After that occasion, she controlled the vibration coming from the strong presence of the Holy Spirit during her prayer.

As hot as a tongue of fire

It is written in Acts 2:3, "They saw what seemed to be tongues of fire that separated and came to rest on each of them." When Jesus was opening the Scripture to the disciples who were heading to Emmaus, they felt their hearts burning (Lk. 24:32). It is obvious that the Holy Spirit came to their hearts.

We may experience our body getting warmer when there is a full presence of the Holy Spirit. We may feel our chest or shoulder or back getting warmer. Some experience their head being electrified. Sometimes there is static electricity on our cheeks, which warms up the back of our neck. The presence of the Holy Spirit through fire can be felt by various parts of our body. However, the presence of the Holy Spirit through fire is sometimes a little too hot or lukewarm.

Sometimes, when I used to lay my hands on someone's head while praying, I felt an electric current running through my hands. When I asked him how he felt, he answered that something hot had penetrated him. But there are people who do not feel the presence of the Holy Spirit at all. They cannot feel it because they are not so very sensitive to the Spirit. Think about the flow of electricity. It flows through substances with metal components. It cannot flow through trees or soil. In a similar manner, if a person is not spiritually prepared, the Holy Spirit cannot penetrate the person. This is why the spiritual attitude of a person being prayed for is so important in experiencing the presence of the Holy Spirit. The Holy Spirit cannot come near a person who is extremely rational or has a negative way of thinking.

The Holy Spirit is a living person who reveals His intentions very clearly to us, such as joy and sadness. Sometimes He reveals Himself to us as fire. He clearly tells us how happy He is through the intensity of fire.

Moses saw a bush burning at Mount Horeb. But that fire did not die nor vanish (Ex. 3:2). It was the Holy God who revealed Himself in a burning bush. Yes, the Holy Spirit is a consuming fire (Deut. 4:24, Heb. 12:29).

People who experienced the fire of the Holy Spirit were lifted up by God to be used as His great and powerful workers. Consider, for example, Reverend Kim, Ik-du's experience of the consuming fire.

Kim, Ik-du was a Presbyterian pastor and a famous revivalist. When he was young he was skeptical of his life and spent his life in fights and drinking. Those who knew him called him 'roughneck Kim.' In 1900, when he was 27 years old, his friend Park Tae-hwan led him to Keumsan church in Anak county. He listened to a sermon on 'eternal life' by American missionary W. L. Swallen and was converted to Christianity. He became a devoted Christian, reading the New Testament 100 times in a year.

In July 1901, Kim Ik-du, his wife and his mother confessed their faith and were baptised by Swallen. After he got baptised, one day, he had to drink reluctantly because his friend wanted him to. While he was drinking he realised that he was sinning so he ran out of that place and went to a mountain. There he cried out to God in repentance. He repented all night long. Early in the morning he came back home and lay down to sleep, and in a dream, he saw a big ball of fire on his chest.

He was so surprised that he shouted "Oh! It's thunder!" Hearing his shriek, his mother ran over to him and woke him up. It was not thunder; it was baptism by fire. From that day on Kim Ik-du became a godly man and started to hate sin and relied only upon the Holy Spirit. Later he went to a seminary and became a pastor. Then he became a great revivalist who built churches in Korea during the Japanese colonial era.

One day, when I was ministering in Brazil, I heard that a group of Brazilian believers was going up a mountain to pray. I also heard that the mountain was kindled every time people prayed. I wanted to see if it was true. So together with a Korean brother I went up the mountain to join the prayer. People arrived on top of the mountain around 1 o'clock in the morning and prayed until 4 o'clock. About 40 people from several churches, men and women, old and young, gathered together and prayed.

About an hour later, something really strange happened. One boy brought a twig to me of which the tip was on fire! When I first saw it, I thought it would be hot so I did not dare touch it. But that boy insisted that I touch it. So at last I touched it. Strangely it was not hot at all. The boy again showed me some leaves on the ground. Those leaves were glowing. I concluded that this phenomenon was the presence of God through the Holy Spirit, just like Moses' burning bush. To remember that day, I took a burning twig and came down the mountain. However, the flame vanished while I was coming down. Every Korean believer in Sao Paulo knows that the mountain burns when Brazilians pray

The presence of the Holy Spirit, like fire, actually occurs when we pray in the fullness of the Spirit. When Augustine was fervently praying in his house, the house suddenly caught fire. Surprised to see the fire, his neighbours hurriedly brought buckets full of water to put out the fire. However, when they reached Augustine's house, they found out that it was not a real fire but the fire of the Holy Spirit.

In the early 1970's, a church in Hongsung caught fire. Villagers saw that the roof of the church was burning so they brought water to put out the fire. But the fire was the fire of the Holy Spirit and because of this many villagers accepted Jesus as their saviour. That church was Hongsung Holiness Church and the senior pastor then was Reverend Song Hyunbin, who was known as a pastor full of the Holy Spirit. Now Hongsung Church has grown into the largest church in that region and his sons, who were raised under their father's spirituality and prayer, are now working as influential pastors in the Holiness church in Korea.

Mystical gifts and miracles

When we are full of the Holy Spirit, we get various "spiritual gifts" and witness "miracles" of the Holy Spirit. According to Acts 2:4, the most typical gift is speaking in tongues. Tongues can be a heavenly language or actual languages of other countries. The disciples in Acts spoke in tongues that were actual languages of other countries. When foreigners heard the disciples speaking in their own languages so fluently, they were stunned (Acts 2:5-12). Joel 2:28-29 says that when the Holy Spirit comes gifts such as "prophecy," "dreams" and "visions" are received by believers. There is a mention of such gifts in 1 Corinthians 12:7-11 as well: the message of wisdom, healing, prophecy, speaking in different kinds of tongues, interpretation of tongues, distinguishing between spirits, and so on.

Fruit of the Holy Spirit

As the Holy Spirit abides within the heart of believers, it is inevitable and natural to bear the fruit of the Holy Spirit (Gal.

5:22-23, Jn. 15:4-5). When we maintain the fullness of the Spirit we automatically bear the fruit of the Spirit. Unlike the fruit of the Holy Spirit, the gifts of the Holy Spirit have nothing to do with maturity of personality and character development; however, the fruit of the Holy Spirit is directly connected to the maturity of our personalities. We cannot tell how mature someone's faith is by the gifts of the Spirit. But through the fruit of the Spirit, we can measure if a believer has true faith and is mature (Mt. 7:20).

What is the difference between Baptism by the Holy Spirit and fullness of the Holy Spirit?

Baptism in the Holy Spirit is different from baptism in water. Baptism in the Holy Spirit is an event of the Holy Spirit coming down and abiding within the person who has accepted Jesus. Through baptism in the Spirit you may or may not experience the gifts of the Spirit. It is the very first event of the Holy Spirit to work in the life of a believer. By His work, the believer's life starts to change.

Baptism in the Holy Spirit is the first step that leads to the fullness of the Spirit. Being in the fullness of the Spirit means to give all of one's life to God. Only the Holy Spirit takes control of us when we are in the fullness of the Spirit. It is very clear that there is a big gap between the baptism in the Spirit and being in the fullness of the Spirit. We should meditate on the Word of God and pray hard in order to be in the fullness of the Holy Spirit. We have to do our best to obey God. Then the Spirit will take full control of our lives. However, being in the fullness of the Spirit is short-lived. It has to be repeated over and over just like we experience ups and downs in the process of achieving sanctification. The truth is that we are most happy when we are filled with the Holy Spirit. And this state allows us to be more devoted and believing in Jesus. That is why Paul told us to be filled with the Spirit (Eph. 5:18).

Letter from the ministry field
Fire from heaven
Sung-woong Song (Chungju Seowon Church. Senior Pastor)

In the 1970s, a small church in the countryside was set on fire by prayer. The whole congregation experienced fire just like the way it happened in Mark's upper room, and many divine gifts were manifested. Even kindergarten and elementary children spoke in tongues and prophesied. The powerful anointing of the Holy Spirit was on the entire congregation. There was powerful divine healing, and people with all kinds of serious diseases got healed. Also, powerful intercessory prayer teams were organised. When they gathered and prayed, demon-possessed people were freed from evil. Along with mysterious powers, the church started to grow explosively.

This church had a revival conference twice a year, in spring and fall. Since it was a rural church, all the town people, even people of other faiths, would come to the revival conference and watch it from outside through the window. It was one of those revival conferences. All the believers came and prayed hard, longing for God's grace. Repentance was witnessed all through that day. They cried, wiped their noses and sweated while they prayed and received grace. Suddenly, there was a great noise outside the church. People of other faiths of the town were making noises. However, the church did not care and continued the conference. When they came out after the conference was over, the town people told them a strange story.

The town people were watching from outside the church. They did not exactly know what was going on in the church, but they heard people clapping, singing, crying and shouting Amen inside. They watched each other with suspicious faces asking why the Jesus freaks were doing such things; was it because they had sinned too much? But suddenly, a huge fireball came down to the church from the sky. The fireball reached one end of the church roof and unfolded itself to cover the whole church building. Then it started to burn the church. Stunned by what they saw, the people called the fire station. And they carried buckets of water to put out the fire. But the fireball rolled up again and flew back into the sky.

The people witnessed these strange happenings in disbelief. After the revival was over, the town people told the church people what had happened in an excited tone. Then they told each other that something strange was going on in the church and that they had decided to believe in Jesus. Afterwards many people of other faiths started to come to the church. The news spread throughout the area and it showed that God is a living God and that the church is a special place. Pastors and believers from the neighboring churches also came to the church and were touched by the Spirit. They went back to their churches and started vigorous prayer movements.

Chapter 5
Finding your potential gift

Generally, there are two kinds of spiritual gifts. One is potential gift and the other is transcendental gift. We are born with individual personalities and talents. Potential gifts are given by the Holy Spirit when He anoints our individual characters and talents. For example, there are gifts of teaching, serving, helping, evangelising, managing, and so on. Every believer has potential gifts in various forms. In this regard, potential gifts can be regarded as general gifts.

When we devote ourselves to the Lord and the Holy Spirit, our undiscovered potential gifts are revealed. There are so many gifts to be listed; singing and playing a musical instrument can be artistic gifts. Driving, cleaning a church and dishwashing can be gifts of serving; evangelising is another gift; taking care of newly-converted believers is a gift of caretaking. These potential and general gifts only shine when one is full of the Holy Spirit. That is the only time when God uses our gifts.

Another kind of gift is transcendental gifts. These gifts are solely given by the supernatural work of the Holy Spirit.

Find your gift
There is a parable of talents in the New Testament. The word *talent* here can be understood as *gift* or *ability*. God has given

everyone the ability to worship Him. Every person has their own unique talent. However, most people do not even know that they have that kind of ability. Sadly, they concentrate on things they are not good at. Myoung-hee Song, a poet, wrote, "God is fair, he gave me what others don't have." How true! God gave us His best gifts. There are gifts that we are aware of and other people also recognise. There are also gifts that are recognised only by us. Also, there are gifts that we do not know that we have, but they are recognised by others. Lastly, there are gifts that are not revealed to anyone including ourselves. What we should do is that we should not envy or be troubled by another person's gift, but rather we should try to find the hidden gift that we have.

When I was a university student, I liked a sister from Jeju Island. I started to write to her. She read my letters and was deeply moved. And we got married. One day she read those letters again. Then turning to me she said, "Your letters caught my heart! And do you know your words have a heart-moving power?" I was quite surprised to hear that. It was then that I learned that I had a talent: I could write.

Gift according to talent
Some people are good at drawing, while others are good at handling machines. Some are good singers, while others have a good memory. Each and every person has various talents given by God. Some people have various talents. Other people have only one distinct talent.

When I was serving a Korean church in America I was a minister for middle school students of the church. The musical condition of the middle school group was really poor. The high school group had a piano, a guitar, a drum set and a bass guitar to use in the service, but the middle school group had none of them, even the commonly used guitar. There was a piano but there was no piano player. By then, the middle school group and high school group were competing with each other and I had to put the middle school group on track. So I bought a guitar first. Then I chose three students who did not know how to play the guitar but were interested in playing it. I asked a church member, who was good at playing the guitar, to teach them. After three months, the middle school group service started to improve. One of the three students who were learning how to play the guitar showed marked improvement. The musical talent hidden in that student was soon discovered.

We can enjoy marvelous blessings of God given to us when we discover our hidden talent and use it to our advantage. Yes, our talent is a gift given to us by God. It would be disbelief not to recognise that God has given us such good gifts.

My daughters were born when I was studying in America. My family had no connections or relatives in America. So my wife had to take care of our children herself. When my first child was born I could not do anything to help my wife gain her strength. I was waited everyday for someone to bring her some food. My heart ached whenever I watched my wife nursing my child without eating well. Then I made up my mind to learn how to cook. First, I started out by learning how to make brown seaweed soup. My cooking skill improved considerably by the time we had our second daughter.

Lastly, when our third child was born, I made brown seaweed soup for my wife, who was in the hospital. I headed to the hospital with my second child on my back, my first child holding my left hand and the soup in my right hand. Taking care of my wife at three childbirths really honed my cooking skill.

My wife soon found a job and looking after the children and doing the house chores became my responsibility. Eventually, I was able to cook brown seaweed soup, bean paste soup, kimchi soup, cold noodles, chicken soup, spicy fish soup, shrimp soup and all other kinds of dishes. Above all, everyone relished eating the stuff I cooked. Well, I discovered my hidden talent for cooking during my study in America. And God loves to make me use my cooking skills often.

I used to make spicy fish soup for fellow believers when I was serving in a small church. The believers relished eating the dishes I cooked. Lunch after Sunday service is very important in a small church. Someone has to cook. Most of the time the pastor's wife has to cook. If you are a good cook, you have to serve your church through your cooking. God loves you more when you do that. The church really needs talented people.

Churches usually have female pianists. But our church had a male pianist. Another male believer was good at handling computers and machines. He installed not only Windows on our church computer, but also a water heater. We looked for him whenever the electricity went out.

One of our sisters was good at giving massage. She could point out why someone was ill just by looking at his or her face and touching the aching part. Many an ailing believer saw her after the service.

Another sister was good at dancing. Vacation Bible school students loved to watch her perform. Our piano player was an image and sound expert as well. He ran a studio downtown. Together with him, I recorded a programme called 'Let's Evangelise' in his studio. I recorded this radio programme with a person whom I had actually evangelised. I had a talk show with that person on how to evangelise non-believers. It was God who used his studio and his recording skill.

Because of this studio experience, it was a lot easier for me to appear in a TV show. My experience was effective when I went out for a CGN TV show last June. Six months of hosting a radio show eased my mind and gave me a lot of poise.

Discover your talents now, for discovering a hidden talent given by God is like finding a hidden treasure (Matt. 13:44).

Gift according to temperament
Our natural temperament is also a God's gift. God uses us as we are. We can succeed in our lives when we know and live by our temperament. Serving in the church will be really effective when we do it based on our temperaments. There are four types of temperaments based on disposition: sanguine, bilious, melancholy and phlegmatic.

People with a sanguine temperament like to do a lot of things. They are passionate and full of love. So they fervently help other people. They have abundant creativity and imagination. They are extrovert and value human relationships.

People with a bilious temperament are brave and progressive. They turn aggressive when they feel they are being subdued. Such people lack patience. They are active and adventurous and have strong will power; they are decisive and self-confident as well.

People with a melancholic temperament pursue perfection. They are analytic and critical. They are good planners, good observers of regulations and very polite. They are self-sacrificial, considerate and faithful; they are gentle and lofty as well.

People with a phlegmatic temperament are calm and obedient. They are self-restrained, self-satisfying, patient and careful. They are generous; they are great listeners as well. Also, they are normally composed and friendly and so prove to be efficient mediators and cooperators.

Of course we cannot classify everyone based on these four types of temperaments. There may be a person who has two or three types of the temperaments evenly. Or there may be a person who has one strong temperament and a little bit of the others. My temperaments are 70 percent bilious and 30 percent sanguine. That is why I have strong driving power and leadership qualities. Also, I like places that offer a good atmosphere, because I am a temperamental person. I am jovial and social as well. My temperaments were really effective in planting and ministering in churches.

My wife is 60 percent phlegmatic and 40 percent melancholic. So she is quiet, speaks only when required and has a strong sense of responsibility. Also, she proved to be an excellent assistant during my last four years of ministering. I thank God for giving me a good wife. Believers have different kinds of temperament. Their religious life is based on their temperaments. If a pastor knows about the temperaments of believers and assigns church work according to their temperaments, the church can become very vital. One of our female believers in the church was 70 percent sanguine. It was not easy to identify her emotions as they changed too often. She was warm-hearted and kind. Also, she was talkative and it was fun to chat with her. Her neighbors and parents from her children's school came to see her very often. She was perfect for the evangelising ministry.

Another female believer was 60 percent phlegmatic and 40 percent melancholic, so she was reticent, calm, orderly and organised. She was stable because she did not act by her feelings. Not so many people came to meet her because she was not social. But once she opened up she would chat freely. Such a believer is ideally suited for training new believers. God uses our temperaments, which are gifts from Him. It is therefore very important to have full knowledge of our temperaments.

Some people often get depressed because they have a melancholic temperament. Such people usually do not know the real cause of their gloominess, but keep trying to get out of their misery. What they need to do is identify their temperament.

Develop your gifts
Our gifts have to be developed. But first we need to know what kind of gift God has given us. Some people live their lives without caring to know what kind of talent and temperament they have. They do not live life to their fullest. Prayer can help you to discover your hidden talent. You also need to exert yourself to develop it.

When I was in school I was keenly interested in singing. It so happened that my voice started breaking when I reached puberty. Strange as it may seem, even after puberty, my voice broke whenever I tried singing high notes. I stayed away from singing high notes and became tone deaf.

This never-a-high-tone attitude to singing and tone-deafness were really awful things for a minister. So I desperately tried to get over my tone deafness. I asked some of the students majoring in music to give me personal music lessons. Among my personal teachers were a student, who is now a Professor of Worship Music at Dongseo University, and the first Korean singer with a visual handicap. They both said that I could never recover my sense of music. I believe God also saw my struggle. Getting rid of my tone deafness was a hard nut to crack. It was during my service at a small church that my efforts bore fruit. The Holy Spirit anointed my efforts, and something miraculous happened to my voice. Yes, our effort and will are critical in developing our gifts.

God helps you when you make efforts to develop your gifts. Prayer is important, but action is absolutely necessary. If you have an ear for music and want to learn to play, let us say, the piano, you will have to take piano lessons. If you want to have an apple, you will have to find a way of getting it. It will not fall into your lap without your making an effort.

Develop your personality
You will have to develop your personality as well. ("This is how I am! "What should I do to improve my personality?") The kind of attitude that accepts your personality as something fixed could be problematic. Our personalities can be developed. You can maximise the strong points of your temperament and supplement your weaknesses. Temperament is a good gift from God. But it is like a rough rock that needs to be polished. Temperament is good material for you to be used by God. Therefore, you need to know your temperament and do your best to get the best out of it.

The most difficult believer while I was pastoring was, in fact, my wife. My progressive, active, extrovert and work-centered personality and my wife's introvert and passive personality always collided. She was against everything I did. She always told me that I had to do everything in an orderly and right manner. She said I should not work as I felt but should make a plan and work by it. It was not a problem for just the two of us. As a senior pastor of a church, that challenge was a huge burden. At first I thought my wife was being too much for me and that she was the one who was pouring cold water on me.

But my wife was right. I definitely needed her negative and critical opinion. I had to work in my own way to enjoy the work, and my wife had to do it right and in an easy manner. It was natural for me and my wife, who have different temperaments, to collide. It was hard for me at the beginning because I thought we were so different. But later I learned that this difference was rather a harmonious relationship that God had given.

The type of people I find the most difficult are people with a melancholic temperament. I just cannot figure out what they are thinking. What I hear from them after I crack a joke and laugh together is that they are tempted because of me. I really do not know what to do about it. However, after I learn about the temperaments, I begin to embrace these melancholic people. I try to accept their temperaments and not to do things that they would not like much. I, as a temperamental person, try not to say needless jokes to melancholic people and stick to 'the right way.' Sometimes I talk through my wife who understands these people well. I do this because I have learned that when people with opposite temperaments talk with each other, there can be misunderstandings I have developed my personality through my ministry. As a result, my life has become very peaceful.

My wife used to have a hard time thinking that her husband was selfish and irresponsible. But she began to understand me. She used to get depressed and timid unconsciously, but she began to try to live joyfully although there was no reason to be happy, just like sanguine people. We became wonderful partners after we both understood each other's temperaments. We were arguing with each other because of our different personalities. But after we accepted each other's temperament, we experienced joy.

This applies to all believers too. They believe in Jesus according to their temperament. So you have to first accept their temperament. And then you have to help them to learn correctly about their temperament. Then you can compliment their strong points and have them do church ministry according to their temperaments. Moreover, you can help them to fix the negative aspects of their temperaments bit by bit. Some believers fight with each other. Basically, they fight because of misunderstandings. It is because they have different personalities and temperaments. As a pastor, you can personally tell them that their personalities are all different. And by doing so, the problems could be solved very easily.

However, you have to know that the negative side of people's personality and temperament cannot be fixed easily. You have to wait until they learn about their temperament. And you have to pray while you wait. When Satan intervenes, the situation becomes irrecoverable even before we can try to make them accept the differences and make up with each other. We have to make effort to develop our temperament. Sanguine people, who persist in their own way, should copy the phlegmatic temperament, which is opposite to theirs. They have to try to take after the phlegmatic temperament's peaceful and patient character and generous and careful disposition. They should also try to listen to what other people say.

On the other hand, phlegmatic people should admire the brave and progressive character of the sanguine temperament. To achieve this, you need to pray. If we pray desperately to change our personality when we know our temperamental problems, God will clearly hear our prayer and solve our problems. Your developed personality and temperament will become a useful tool to be used by God. People with various temperaments come to church. Do you know how happy it is to have so many different temperaments? Being different is good. It is good to be new to each other. But when our temperament changes in the Holy Spirit, we get a chance to experience joy.

Gifts anointed by the Holy Spirit

We need God's help even after developing our talents and temperament. It is very clear that human effort is absolutely required and that God uses human effort. But we have to know that there is a limit to human effort. Professor Dong-il Han, who is now Professor at the music school of Boston University and regarded as a genius, once felt he would never be able to play the piano well. So he did not touch the piano for a year. He was worn out after putting forth his efforts. This is why we must walk with the Holy Spirit so that He anoints our efforts. Exodus 31:3 shows that Bezalel and Oholiab were filled with the Spirit of God. Amazing things happen when the Holy Spirit anoints; our efforts and our talents merge and we experience great joy.

Miracle for a tone-deaf person

Like I said, I was tone deaf. But I never lost hope. I knew that sooner or later God would change my voice and I continued making efforts while waiting for the miracle to happen.

When I was serving in Gae-bong church in Seoul in the late 1980s, I saw a deaconess who sang really well, as if she had majored in music. She said her voice suddenly changed when the Holy Spirit came upon her. I immediately started praying for a similar miracle in my life. Strange as it may seem, I met one more person in America who had received the gift of singing. My hope knew no bounds. The hope that God would someday answer my prayer greatly helped me in overcoming the suffering caused by my being tone deaf.

One day I felt that my voice had improved a little bit so I asked my wife, "Honey! Don't you think my voice has changed?" My wife answered, "Well! It's the same as usual." But I was not disappointed. Although I emitted pig-squealing sounds, I regarded myself as a good singer and this made it a lot easier when practicing singing. Hope for the anointing of the Holy Spirit was really a source of big strength for a pastor who was ashamed of being tone deaf.

During those days I also noticed that my voice changed when I sang in the fullness of the Holy Spirit. I first found this out when my wife told me, "Honey! Your praise today was very graceful." But whenever I tried to sing a song for someone else, the quality of my voice deteriorated.

Thirteen years of anxious waiting for the anointing of the Holy Spirit had passed, and finally an answer came. It happened when I was ardently pastoring a church after planting it. Now I could sing in full-throated ease. I could also sing high notes. Those who knew me were surprised to see me singing. I proudly proclaimed that the Holy Spirit had anointed my voice.

Yearning for a gift of preaching
Well-known pastors came to our seminary to give challenging sermons in chapels. Their sermons were meaningful, but I was more impressed with overall quality of the speeches. "How do they manage to preach so gracefully?" I wondered.

So I decided to go to many churches. I went to Onnuri Church, Sarang Church, Somang Church, Gwangnim Church, Calvary Church, Myoungsung Church and many other churches and listened to the sermons delivered by famous pastors. While listening to those high-quality sermons, I earnestly prayed to God: "God! Make me preach just like them." I could not think of emulating them without God's help. I did write sermons and delivered them whenever I had a chance, and I was not bad.

However, I felt that there was a qualitative difference. Although people told me that they were touched by my sermons, I could not shake off the miserable feeling that plagued me. My sermons did not change when I was serving a Korean church in America, and during my service as an assistant pastor in Latin America, I wanted to become a pastor like Dongwon Lee, Yongjo Ha and Samhwan Kim. Believers told me they were touched and I was glad to hear that. But this joy was temporary. I knew there was an absolute difference and I could not stop yearning for the anointing of the Holy Spirit. I tried for it for 12 years. And then I planted a church and started to preach several times a week. But I found preaching rather hard, and I just could not figure out why. I found the morning sermon really difficult to deliver. The afternoon sermon was quite easy. Some kind of a heavy atmosphere prevailed over the Sunday morning service and I was not able to change that atmosphere.

One year passed like that. A male believer came to me and said, "Pastor, there is no change in your sermon. The Sunday sermon is always the same." His words really hit the nail on the head. I became very anxious on every Saturday and I was afraid of Sundays. Actually, I thought I was delivering challenging sermons, but I could not figure out why that believer found the sermons repetitive.

But it was true and I had to admit it. I worried and suffered, and one day, the anointing of the Holy Spirit finally came upon me. It was on a Sunday two years after I had planted the church. The faces of the believers became brighter as I delivered the sermon. I said something and they broke into laughter. It was so strange. It was the first time that I found delivering a sermon easy. I am not saying that anyone can do this when there is the anointing of the Holy Spirit. I think we should acquire the skills of preaching and earnestly study the Bible in order to make our preaching more effective.

However, this is not enough. Preaching differs when there is spiritual ability. This is how Pastor Moody, who did not even graduate from elementary school, revolutionarily changed millions of Americans with the Word of God in the nineteenth century. Now I feel that I can freely preach the Word. I can feel people being touched and being changed. It was after 14 years of ardent prayer for a gift of preaching, that the Holy Spirit came to me.

Use your gift for God

Our talent is not ours. It is given to us by God. Therefore, it has to be used in the service of God. We are just His stewards. The master of my voice is God and if I have a good voice, I should serve the church through a choir. If you are a good writer, you should write good novels and poems to praise God. We should use our talents to give glory to God. Of course, it is true that we run our lives through our gifts. If you are a comic artist, you have to earn money by selling your drawings. If you are a cook, you have to earn money by running a restaurant or working as a chef. But the ultimate purpose of your gift is to glorify the name of God. Serve the church while you are working to earn money. Do not forget that serving God comes before your job. God will feel sorry if your priority changes. Perhaps the connection of your talent to your profession might be the calling of God for you.

God has called you to be a cobbler, comic artist, computer graphic designer, writer or school teacher. We must be faithful to God's calling. But, we must also know the purpose of the calling. God has called us to give glory to Him and to commit ourselves to Him. Especially, those whose talents have been anointed by the Holy Spirit have to even more deeply commit themselves to God for His glory.

It so happened that soon after I learned that my voice had been anointed by the Spirit, I unconsciously became arrogant. I felt strange whenever I hit a chord in a high tone. I was proud of myself. I found myself unconsciously enjoying myself when someone listened to my singing and praised me for it. We must remember that God takes away the anointing if someone uses the "gift" to honor himself instead of God.

Therefore, we have to use our "gifts" and the anointing of our gifts by the Holy Spirit only for the church and for Jesus Christ. We must not become arrogant. Arrogance would only make us fall like the archangel Lucifer and King Saul. The Holy Spirit anoints your "gift" because you have been called to witness Jesus Christ. People would be surprised to see your very special gift. You should tell others about Jesus through your "gift."

Chapter 6
Seeking gifts of the Holy Spirit

Gifts of the Holy Spirit are gifts poured onto us by God for the benefit of believers and the entire church community. The most common gift we can see is the gift of tongues. But there are also gifts such as prophecy, interpretation, vision, healing and casting out demons. These are rare gifts.

Transcendental gifts of the Holy Sprit are supernatural gifts given to us by God and these gifts are something that we did not have before. These transcendental gifts are warmly welcomed in the Pentecostal church. But most of the traditional churches are skeptical about these gifts. They say gifts of the Holy Spirit are already over in the apostolic era. Pastors of these churches do not allow praying in tongues in early morning prayer meetings and even send a new believer to another church if the believer prays in tongues. Pastors of traditional churches denounce gifts of the Holy Spirit and lay stress only on the authority of the Bible. They do everything they can to nurture believers. To them, it is the Bible that matters the most. The emphasis is on efficiency, safety and continuity of discipleship training through the Bible. They never overlook the dangers of the gifts of the Holy Spirit, such as tongues, prophecies, visions, divine healing, casting out demons and others. But their apprehension is understandable because throughout history, people who have had strong gifts of the Holy Spirit have become leaders of heresy. A well-known example is elder Taeseon Park of Jundogwan. He said prophesying at church sometimes causes disorder and confusion in the church. Sometimes believers follow the one who has received a strong gift of the Holy Spirit instead of their minister. Moreover, the one who has received the gift stands against the minister to tell believers that he or she has heard God's voice or seen a vision. In fact, people with the gift of the Holy Spirit could take pride in themselves when they are not in the fullness of the Spirit.

However, there are churches that have been revived by welcoming and using the gifts of the Holy Spirit well. They include Pentecostal churches like Yeouido Full Gospel Church, Methodist, Holiness and Baptist churches. Also, there are Presbyterian churches that welcome and use such gifts. The explosive growth of Yeouido Full Gospel Church from 1970 to 1980 can be ascribed to Pastor Yonggi Cho's use of his gift of divine healing. While listening to Pastor Cho's sermons, believers were healed of cancer, lung disease, stomach disease, and so on. A person who had infantile paralysis and came with crutches walked out without them after listening to the sermon. They experienced the dynamic working of the Holy Spirit that the churches in Acts witnessed ages ago.

Korean churches are undergoing sharp conflict concerning the gifts of the Holy Spirit. The traditional church warns of the danger of the gifts of the Holy Spirit and focuses on faith based on the Bible. The other is the Pentecostal church that emphasises the gifts of the Holy Spirit but is careless about discipleship training through the Bible. One is a faith focusing on reason and the other is a faith focusing too much on emotion. Is there a way of combining the strong points of both—the traditional church that emphasises the Bible and the Pentecostal church that emphasises the gifts of the Holy Spirit?

If the gifts of the Holy Spirit are clearly gifts from God, then they surely will give us benefits. And we must use those gifts wisely. Now I am going to analyse these supernatural gifts based on my experience. I would focus on gifts such as tongues, prophecy, vision, divine healing and casting out of demons.

Tongues—heavenly languages

We are not unfamiliar with the gift of tongues because quite a few of us have prayed in tongues. Tongues are one of the gifts of the Holy Spirit. But this is not the only gift or the most significant gift. That is why all believers have not prayed in tongues.

Tongues do not prove that a person is in the fullness of the Spirit. One can be filled with the Holy Spirit without having tongues. However, tongues are a supernatural phenomenon that happens when we experience the Holy Spirit. Tongues make us experience the supernatural work of the Spirit.

We can consider tongues as heavenly languages because we speak in a language that sounds strange. Some tongues are Chinese, French, or English. Sometimes tongues may sound like the mumblings of a lunatic. Here is an interesting story. One female believer started praying in tongues just when she was about to be sexually assaulted. Mistaking her for a crazy woman, the criminal left her.

A sad story about tongues

We can easily see people praying in tongues. But, at times, we envy the recipients of tongues, if we have not ever prayed in tongues. Of course people who deny tongues do not envy those who have received them.

When I was young, I went to a Pentecostal church that emphasised tongues. Every night at 9 o'clock twenty to thirty people gathered at the church to pray together. I joined the prayer meeting as the son of a pastor when I was a middle-school student. And I desperately wanted to receive the gift of tongues.

As the son of a pastor, I was embarrassed because I could not pray in tongues, while almost all of the people I knew prayed in tongues. So I cried out to God. "O Lord, help me! I want to speak in tongues!" Three depressing years passed without my receiving the "gift" from the Holy Spirit. I had to put up with all the pain. People said to me, "God will give it to you if you ask for it. Pray harder!"

Their advice made me sad. When I became a high school student, I could no more go to those prayer meetings because I had not received tongues. No one said "You shouldn't come," but I felt alienated and could not go. So I started to pray alone in a small room. Time passed. I was in my last year of high school. It was winter and I got accepted to a theological university. Soon I was obsessed with the thought that I must receive tongues because I would be a theological student. "Only students with good faith will come to the theological school …what am I supposed to do? I can't even pray in tongues!" I wondered. So I asked my parents to pray for me to get tongues. But even that did not work.

Eventually, I received tongues in a student retreat when I was in my second year of school. But my tongues were going *la-la-la*. I was so grateful to receive this precious gift. But there was a problem. Students living in the dormitory were having early morning worship and when the service was over, all of them were praying fluently in tongues.

I could not pray for even a second with my *la-la-la* tongues. So I prayed in a low voice or would come out of the chapel and pray in a quiet place. I blamed God for it.

"God, give me some nice tongues? You hurt my pride!"

For a long time I suffered from the "tongues-complex." I still face the same problem. The tongues I spoke changed a little bit, but I was not happy, as they went *olode kelodi*. Everyone could mimic my tongues. One day, Sunday school children came along with their mothers to attend an adult prayer meeting. They chuckled when they heard my tongues and laughingly did what they called "Pastor's tongues play."

Well, I still pray in those tongues: *olode kelodi*. No, I do not want to give up my tongues because people make fun of them. It took me years to get them.

The gift of tongues continues

Some people say believers ceased to receive gifts of the Holy Spirit, such as tongues, after the apostles' age and so there are no such things as gifts of the Holy Spirit in today's world. They do not let people pray in tongues in their churches.

If what they say is true, what should we do about people praying in tongues nowadays? Are they demon possessed? Should we consider tongues as gifts of the Holy Spirit?

I believe that it is still possible to receive gifts of the Holy Spirit. Ours is the age of the church, which is the age of the Holy Spirit. The Holy Spirit is still alive, and if He is alive, believers will continue to receive spiritual gifts.

Speaking in tongues has a biblical basis. Paul acknowledged it. He advised us not to forbid tongues (1Co. 14:39). He strongly advised us to use tongues in order to build up personal spirituality and virtue (1Co. 14:4). However, we should not pray in tongues if the church is having an official meeting. This is because the virtue of a church can be built when praying in languages that people can understand instead of praying in tongues that people cannot (1 Co. 14:23).

Also, we might scare people of other faiths if we pray in tongues with them. Therefore, we should be wise enough to choose the right time and place to pray in tongues.

What are demon-possessed tongues?
I have seen many people praying in demonic tongues. Believers usually cannot tell the difference between holy tongues and demonic tongues. The characteristic of demonic tongues is that they are very loud when praying. People who are possessed by demons sometimes jerk their hands and feet as if they were crazy. And there are people who pray more gently than them.

I get confused and my prayer is blocked when I pray with those who pray in demonic tongues. A person praying in demonic tongues injects a lot of hatred and fear into a genuine prayer meeting, thus disrupting the meeting abruptly. This happens because such a person disturbs the people praying in the meeting by instilling spiritual hostility in them. Only those with spiritual discernment and authority can prevent a prayer meeting from being a complete fiasco.

How do people acquire demonic tongues? A demon invades especially those who are in a state of shock or afflicted by fear. A demon gives tongues to the person whom it possesses. This is why we must not go up a mountain to pray. We must also avoid going to a prayer house alone in the dark. Demons suddenly attack us when we are scared while praying alone and give us demonic tongues. We must remember that holy tongues and demonic tongues are opposite to each other in every way.

What should we do when we see people praying in demonic tongues?

Pastors or church leaders with strong spiritual discernment must quickly separate people praying in demonic tongues from the believers. In order to do this, they need to pray even more earnestly to obtain greater spiritual power. The human relationships maintained by the demon-possessed person also need to be considered. There is no doubt that the demon will maintain its position through those relationships. People who know the demon-possessed person will also be tempted. This is why we should be as wise as a serpent.

We learn about the nature of evil spirits through this spiritual warfare. Through all this, the church is strengthened and believers are empowered with stronger spiritual power. In other words, they get to learn how to use spears, swords and shields through experiencing warfare. In fact, demon-possessed tongues are not mentioned in the Bible. Sometimes it could cause trouble to an innocent person. Let us say someone hates another person in a church. When the person that he does not like prays in tongues, an evil spirit can work to make him think that the person is praying in demon-possessed tongues. This is why we should not condemn a person as having demon-possessed tongues and alienate him or her from the community. The work of the Holy Spirit and the work of evil spirits can be naturally discerned when a minister and a community stay close to each other for a long time.

What are tongues good for?
Tongues are spiritual prayers offered to God (2Co. 14:2). They can be regarded as prayers of the spirit within us to God who is the Spirit. Tongues enable us to pray to God in heavenly languages. They make us express what we cannot express in our own language.

Through tongues, our spirit prays to God and we can tell God of our conditions in detail. We sometimes lose our strength and cannot do anything when we are in so much pain. Tongues can help us at a time like this. We experience our spirit being restored when we pray in tongues without depending on our thoughts. As we pray in tongues, God sometimes gives us strength to pray.

Tongues are also helpful in urgent situations. We might not pray a word when we see a fellow believer being sent to the hospital due to a heart attack because we are greatly shocked. But, the gift of tongues enables us to constantly pray for the believer.

The gift of tongues is a gift for an individual rather than a community or church (1Co. 14:4). We sometimes find it difficult to pray for ourselves or for other people at church because people next to us can hear our prayers. Praying in tongues is very useful when we have to pray for something that needs to be kept as a secret. It is very effective to pray both in tongues and thought (1Co. 14:15). The most important benefit we can get from having tongues is that through tongues we can receive other gifts of the Holy Spirit. Tongues are the first step towards experiencing various gifts, such as the gifts of interpretation, prophecy, vision, divine healing, casting out demons, etc. We can receive these gifts without having tongues, but normally these gifts come after receiving the gift of tongues.

Tongues are a gift of the Holy Spirit. But tongues are not the only gift. This is a gift that benefits an individual's spirituality. People who do not receive tongues can also be in the fullness of the Holy Spirit. Tongues have nothing to do with our salvation. Therefore, we can become a powerful Christian by using tongues well.

However, there are a few more steps we need to take. We need spiritual discernment after we enter the spiritual world. A new convert could encounter many dangers when suddenly experiencing mystical events. The convert will have to meet a spiritual leader who can give guidance. It is necessary to have a spiritual leader with discernment and friends who can journey along in the spiritual world praying together in order to manage the life of faith well.

Prophecy—a spiritual discernment

Although Satan does not follow God, he knows a lot about Him and His son, Jesus. Satan and evil spirits also have a good idea of the future of humans, for they are the ones who help diviners or shamans tell the future (Act.16:16). Satan seduces people into taking the easy road. He tempts them to follow him instead of God.

The Bible tells us that when the Holy Spirit comes to us we prophesy and see visions (Jo. 2:28-32). As promised, the Holy Spirit came and the apostles were filled with the Holy Spirit and spoke in tongues and prophesied. Relying on the Holy Spirit, Paul prophesied the future of the people who came on board with him (Act. 27:10). It was an angel who foretold their future to Paul (Act. 27:23-24).

Anyone who is in the fullness of the Spirit can prophesy (Num. 11:24-29). Demons speak to one who is demon-possessed. In the same way, the Holy Spirit speaks to those who are in the fullness of the Spirit.

Who is prophesying now?

Cindy Jacobs from America is renowned for her ministry of prophecy. It is known that she sometimes prophesies the destiny of countries and nations. Her ministry is targeted at kings and presidents. It is a common fact that she prophesied the unification of Germany. She visited Korea this year and had an assembly in the Olympic Hall with 7,000 Christians. Hundreds of people had to go back because there were not enough seats. This is a good example of Korean churches showing interest in prophetical ministry.

In fact, there are also many prophets in Korea. I have met at least 20 people who can prophesy. Prophets are those who are filled with the Holy Spirit. When the Holy Spirit comes to you, it not only leads you, but also enables you to prophesise. That is the promise of Jesus (Jn. 16:13).

If you choose to follow the Holy Spirit, the Spirit will touch you and give you feelings about the future. My wife prophesies when she is in the fullness of the Holy Spirit. But she tries not to tell and even controls it because she is a quiet and calm person. In our church, there is a deacon named Sangdeok Kim. He is a worship-leader and plays the guitar. One day, in 1997, my wife went to a prayer meeting in Jecheon. That evening my wife first met Deacon Kim and she prayed for him. He was having back pain at that time and was wondering whether he should join the army or not. My wife prayed and told him that he would be discharged from the army right after getting enlisted. After that, he joined the army and went to a training camp in Chuncheon, Gangwondo. There he was assessed to be exempted from military service, and he got discharged. This became an occasion for us to get closely related. He came to our church when he moved to Seoul and has been leading the worship ever since. Hearing God's voice is a marvelous experience.

How do we prophesy?

Prophets usually pray in tongues and interpret the tongues afterwards—that is how they prophesy. Their prayers in tongues and interpretations naturally connect in prophecies. When they pray for a certain person, they feel it in their heart;

they hear voices and sometimes see through visions. Some other prophets prophesy directly through normal language. Their lives are prayer and they just hear the voice of God or see visions when they start to pray.

One day, in March 2005, my wife and I were staying up all night praying at our church. I was writing a book titled *Jesus! He is Coming* at that time. In the early morning, my wife said to me,

"Honey! God said that he will greatly use your book."

"Yes!" I replied—my heart touched.

She said that God spoke to her in His voice.

Just as my wife had heard, God's message really did come true. Three months later, the book was published, and strangely, after two weeks, it was introduced as a topic book in Kookmin Newspaper. A Christian broadcast station soon called me and asked for an interview. Another marvelous thing happened. Our church was going to have a worship meeting. Mrs. Kyoung-ju Chung, who was a worship minister of Far East Broadcasting Station, was invited. This happened right after the book had been published, and the book was naturally introduced through the broadcast station. The book really sold well. That is what God had planned for me.

The true meaning of prophecy

God tells us about our future, but He seldom does that (Ecc. 7:14). We cannot tell what will happen in our future life (Ecc. 8:7, 9:1). We just have to depend on God in every moment of our lives.

God always reveals His plan to us. This is how He works. We want to know everything about His plan, but this is our desire. Also, our life will lose its meaning if we fully learn about God's plan all at once. A relationship of strong love with God will also be useless. God is willing to launch His plans for us one at a time.

Prophecy can be understood as having an insight into God's plan for us. It is all about hearing the voice of the Holy Spirit and having an intimate relationship with the Spirit (1Co. 14).

Benefits of the gift of prophecy

The benefit of having the gift of prophecy is that you can learn about God's plan for you. We feel relieved when we learn about God's plan for us. The gift of prophecy enables us to have a vision and follow it.

From early 2006, I felt that God was speaking to me about my course. But I did not know what it was and sometimes I was even nervous about it. When I was about to finish my seminary, I started to fast in the morning from June 1st to 20th. I wanted God to tell me about my future.

The day before the last day of my morning fasting, my friend, who was a pastor serving as a staff at our denomination's missions department, called me. He was asking me to interpret at a denominational general assembly. I refused it several times because I did not feel confident of my English skills. But he did not listen to me. Before I came out of my house, my wife and I prayed for good interpretation. After the prayer, my wife told me, "God will make you happy." By God's grace, my performance on that day was quite impressive. O how my heart pounded with excitement that night!

The next morning I went to a working-level meeting between the head of our mission office and Mr. David Long, the president of OMS, for interpretation. While I was interpreting in the meeting, which dealt with detailed plans for world missions, I felt my heart strangely warmed. Then

Seeking gifts of the Holy Spirit

I questioned myself, "Why has God sent me to a meeting for world missions?"

I had lunch with President David Long that afternoon, and while we were having a conversation, a strange thought raced through my mind: "Do I have to go out as a missionary again?"

I was in a seminary ministry in 1993 in Moscow with American missionaries from OMS. I recalled teaching Russian seminary students together with Harold Brown and Steven Loid, and I talked about this with President Long. Having a personal meeting with the OMS president was really an honor for me.

> "I never thought I would come to a general assembly of our denomination," I said to myself.
> God's providence and guidance are immense.

And then I talked with the chairman of the Evangelical Church of India. He has been serving as the chairman of ECI with over 3,000 churches. I gave him my book that was published in America and I saw him reading it in his free time. Then he told me that the idea contained in my book came very close to Indian ideology. He showed interest in me, and I felt some kind of an intimacy towards him.

I prayed to God: "God, do you want me to go to the mission field?" I was challenged to go out as a missionary in my heart, but I was also scared. I was obedient to God's call and I had moved around the globe eight times, but then I felt I could not do it anymore. I felt that I had become old. In my fearless 20s and 30s, I moved around here and there. But as I was about to reach the age of 40, I instinctively desired stability. I had a strong desire to stay and settle down in Korea. And I worried what would happen if God told me to go abroad again. But I was thinking that I had to obey God's call. Then I said to myself, "I will go if he tells me to go!"

That afternoon I made an urgent phone call to the person I always talk to whenever I face a problem. It was a pastor named Myoung-hun Yoon. Pastor Yoon is a 62-year-old woman. She is always praying and is sensitive to the voice of God. She is currently serving in Faith Methodist Church in Seoul. Pastor Yoon got her Doctor of Ministry degree at Mokwon University and she is intellectually inclined. She is also a trusted minister who served twice as chairman of the female ministers' mission committee of Seoul southern association. I thanked God for letting me have a spiritual relationship with a pastor like her. I was very serious so I asked her the question that had been troubling me:

"Pastor! God wants me to go abroad as a missionary. What do I do about this?"

"You should go if God told you to go. Don't you think?" she answered.

After praying for me, she said:

"God says you should go to India."

I had not mentioned anything in detail. But Pastor Yoon knew where I was supposed to go. She pointed out the exact place—India. It was God who had told her about it. For a moment I was speechless when I heard that. Several thoughts ran through my mind:

I was having dinner interpreting what the ECI president was saying last night...

I talked with him at the denominational meeting today and he was reading my book all day...

He said that the idea of my book matched that of India very well ...

I thought that God was telling me to go to India, a country I had never thought about... That night, I went to a hotel where the members of the general assembly were staying.

There I talked all through the night with the head of the missions department of our denomination and a missionary who was on the mission field in Indonesia. I carefully asked contrast, there were too many professors in Korea. Pastors in India could not receive proper training because of this problem. Then they told me that I was the right person to do seminary ministry there. Listening to what they said warmed my heart again.

God answered me when I was fasting in the morning for 20 days. He spoke to me through my environment and the people I met. God also spoke to me through Pastor Yoon's prophecy. It was not Pastor Yoon's prophecy that decided my future steps. It just added more assurance to the process of my learning about God's plan.

I am preparing to leave for India as a missionary, so I am calmly solving the issues related to my forthcoming visit. Surprisingly, I feel much better now—mainly because I am following God's plan for me. Many surprising things have happened ever since I made up my mind to go to India, which prove that God wants me to make this visit. First of all, the problem of my successor in the church has been solved easily. One church wanted to support a missionary, and its condition of support was that the mission had to be 'Indian mission.' So, naturally, I was connected to it. Also, when the Head of our missions department was inspecting the mission fields in China, he met an American missionary named Kilbourne, who asked him to send a professor to an Indian seminary, which would open in early 2007. The Head of the missions department told me that he thought of me when he heard the missionary's request.

Problems with the gift of prophecy
The gift of prophecy gives very special benefits. But it also causes many problems. Believers tend to think only of the

good side of prophecy. They do not know well enough how dangerous it could be. The gift of prophecy is like a fire that could cause disaster unless it is well controlled. Fire under good control can be used to cook delicious food. But if it is carelessly handled, it could become extremely dangerous.

Suppose you ask a prophecy minister about God's will. The minister tells you about God's plan for you. It is really wonderful and convenient, but there is all likelihood of your getting addicted to the wonder and convenience. You may unconsciously get into the habit of seeing a prophet each time you face a problem. You may slowly deconstruct your behavior of carefully listening to God's voice while praying. You may start depending more on the minister than on God.

One day, you will try to find another prophet if you feel that the former prophet is no longer spiritual and not as good as before. You have become nothing more than a worldly man who goes to see a fortune teller. In a similar manner, the gift of prophecy could make a believer depend too much on prophecy. Such a believer may become nervous about his future if he misses prophetic prayers even for a day.

Another problem that you may encounter after receiving the gift of prophecy is that you may unconsciously become arrogant. You may take pride in yourself when you tell people about their future. You start to reign over people without knowing what you are doing. And you may think that the gift was originally yours and ask people to give you something or pay you in return for your prophecy for them. These things can happen if there is a lack of proper understanding of the gifts of the Holy Spirit.

In this case, the gift would not last long. And an evil spirit would come and cover up the glory of God through this gift. Because the gift of prophecy is so dangerous, there are not so many prophets who maintain this gift. This is why many prophets give up their ministry and vanish or go the way of heresy.

There was a young enthusiastic minister who prayed a lot. On November 11, 1952, he built a cabin on a small island and started to fast and pray to remove his sinful nature. He was already leading a religious life, becoming one with God through asceticism rather experiencing God through the Bible. He said that he heard a spiritual voice saying "Do you love me?" on November 30, 1952. He answered in accordance to what was written in the Bible. He said that there was a clear sign of the Taeguk symbol on a rock where he had put his head while praying. He believed that the sign proved him to be a global leader. After that, on June 13, 1953, while he was praying and fasting for 40 days in his prayer cabin, he said he was possessed by a stream of heavenly light. He said that he received divine power in his hand. He then fell into extreme mysticism.

Then on March 1, 1964, he received a divine revelation while praying at Bethel Prayer House in Kwanak Mountain, and he started the 'House of God' movement. In August of the same year, he went to Kyeryong Mountain and considered the mountain as the primary place for his national mission. There he wore white clothes with a gold crown on his head and rode a white horse and regarded himself to be the savior and messiah of his nation and the world. He is pastor Do-cheon Yang of the World Religion Committee. We must not forget the fact that people who take God's direct revelation seriously can be possessed by demons.

Another problem that can be caused by the gift of prophecy is that prophecies are not always right. Prophets sometimes give absurd prophecies. When they do that they get discouraged, and the person who was prayed for by the prophet gets disappointed. Their prophecies have to be correct all the time; sometimes they are so surprisingly correct, while sometimes they are not. This is why the mysterious aspect of prophecy always has to be harmonised with our reason. On this point, prophecy ministers must receive some guidance.

In the 1960s, a very strange prophecy spread in D church in Daejeon. The source was unclear but among the believers a prophecy saying "misfortune is coming and we should escape to Jeju Island" was spreading. During that time the church was filled with the Holy Spirit and through praying day and night they received all kinds of gifts of the Spirit, including the gift of prophecy. They did not doubt the prophecy because it was always correct. Soon the church was disturbed. Fifteen families left for Jeju Island, and the rest doubted and did not believe the prophecy. As time passed, the prophecy turned out to be a lie. Clearly, they were tricked by an evil spirit.

It is very obvious that the gift of prophecy has to be carefully approached. We have to remember that the work of the Holy Spirit and the work of evil spirits always coexist. Therefore, we should be equipped with spiritual discernment and realistic rational judgment.

Cautions when using the gift of prophecy

Firstly, if you have the gift of prophecy, your behaviour must be modest. You always have to admit that the gift belongs to the Holy Spirit. It is the Holy Spirit that works through you. You will become nothing when the Holy Spirit takes away your gift. Do not misunderstand that you will always have that gift throughout your life. We cannot own the gift of the Holy Spirit. The gift belongs solely to the Spirit. Therefore, whenever you use the gift, you must acknowledge this fact and be modest. It is very clear that if you take pride in yourself about having a gift, you will invite evil spirits.

Secondly, prophecy should be used only as a supplement to the Word of God. How could we entrust our fate to the prophecy prayer of one person? This could be a foolish act. Would you like to base everything on a prophecy that you heard one day? When prophecy is given by other people or you yourself have received it, it must be verified with the Bible. Also, it has to be examined with spiritual discernment. Moreover, we should consider it with our reasoning. The gift of prophecy should be understood in the light of references and supplementary aspects. First of all, we should obtain the essential inspiration through the Word of God. Then we should listen to God's voice through our surrounding environment. And when the gift of prophecy is added upon this as a reference, then we will be able to wholly listen to the voice of God.

Let us say a person does not love to hear the Holy Spirit's voice through the Bible but seeks God's will only through the gift of prophecy. He is, then, liable to be deceived by an evil spirit.

Thirdly, we should not ignore or deny the gift of the Holy Spirit because a prophecy sounds absurd and strange. It is not the Holy Spirit's gift that is wrong, but it is because we are weak and an evil spirit has tricked us. There are ministers who deny these gifts because of these problems. We may regard them as arrogant ministers. We have to admit not only the Word of God, but also the work of the Holy Spirit who works in so many different ways. You should know that these gifts of the Spirit can greatly help your ministry if you have a healthy theology and your faith stands upon the Word of God.

Fourthly, you should control the prophecy that you have received. There is a temptation of speaking of the voice and vision you have heard and seen. Prophecy about you or about other people always has to be treated with great concern. That prophecy might have come out of your emotion. Evil spirits can take advantage of it. Therefore, it may be more helpful to control the temptation to speak and quietly watch what will happen. I have come across many cases where people were tempted when they spoke about prophecy and visions without filtering them. We should filter things that are of no good in building virtue and express those that can be helpful (1Co. 14:4). Never forget that there is always an evil spirit that is vigilantly looking for a small gap to break in where there is a powerful work of the Holy Spirit.

Fifthly, the most ideal way to use the gift of prophecy is to pray together with people who have received various other gifts and discern it with each other (1Co. 14:29-33). It could be even more effective when a minister who is equipped with spiritual discernment and theological training joins the prayer and controls the balance. That minister has to control the balance between God's Word and the Holy Spirit's gifts. The prayer meeting will not last long if the people do not study the Bible and just focus on pursuing mysterious voices and visions. I would say it is best to have a prayer meeting to share the gift of prophecy, interpreting and discerning it, once a week. Prayer meetings other than that should be for intercession, praise and worship and Bible study and for focusing all of these on people's lives.

Visions, God's will

God gives us visions when we pray. Peter saw a vision when he was praying (Act. 10:9-16). Paul also gave up going to Asia for a mission after seeing a vision of Macedonia, and he headed for Europe (Act. 16:6-10). The Holy Spirit speaks to us through visions. Visions are part of the gift of the Holy Spirit.

Seeking gifts of the Holy Spirit

One day, in April of 2006, I visited a house of a believer who had given birth to her second child four months ago. She said she was feeling gloomy. It was understandable. She was exhausted from breast-feeding her second child while taking care of her first son as well. Her problem was her four-year-old son. She said earlier he was behaving himself, but now he was acting like an infant. Her body was also worn out and she was feeling disappointed with her son. My wife and I comforted her, telling her that all babies are the same, just like her child. Then we had a worship service for her family.

She cried while attending the service. She cried because she was so deeply moved. She said she saw a vision for the first time in her life: A message appeared in white letters on a black screen just like in the movies. It read "I love you my daughter!" She was deeply touched by the words of God.

With our spiritual ears we could listen to God's voice, and with our spiritual eyes we could see visions given by the Holy Spirit. God is so liberal that he speaks to us through everything we have. Therefore, we have to acknowledge God's power and freedom to speak to us through our eyes, ears and mind.

One Sunday, on July 9th, 2006, one of our youth members in our church gave me a book. The moment I received the book I felt like writing a book on the Holy Spirit. On the following day, in a prayer meeting, another believer told me about a vision he had seen.

"Pastor, you were holding a pen and writing something on a large piece of paper."

When I heard that I made up my mind that I should write a book on the Holy Spirit. I did not make up my mind to write a book about the Spirit through that vision. I already had the thought of writing a book in my mind, and I felt that the Holy Spirit was guiding me on that. I was electrified in my mind when the young man handed me the book, and when the believer told me about the vision, I was convinced that I had to write a book on the Holy Spirit.

Someone was praying and suddenly his spiritual eyes were opened and he saw a vision of a series of subtitles just like in the movies. A vision is truly a mysterious gift, but at the same time it is also a dangerous gift. What is the difference between a vision that you have seen and a vision that a lunatic has seen? How will you explain your vision to a person of other faith? How can you prove that the vision you saw is from the Holy Spirit? What will you do when an evil spirit takes advantage of your vision?

To tell the truth, I do not have gifts of visions or prophecy. But this does not mean that I do not have any spiritual gifts. I can discern works of the Holy Spirit and evil spirits. I also have rational and historical insight that can harmonise naturalness and super-naturalness, reason and super-reason. Perhaps that is why I can observe, analyse and organise these mysterious gifts and build up a theological structure about them.

The gift of visions can be very real when we are in the fullness of the Word, grace and prayer. It can greatly affect our decisions and future and give practical help to us. However, there are some dangers when we deal with the gift of visions. How should we deal with this gift? This is truly a troublesome matter for those who yearn to have the gift.

How should we deal with the gift of vision?
What should we do if we keep seeing visions while praying? Some might not be able to bear the visions coming from the Holy Spirit. One new believer was ardently praying at a

church. Suddenly mysterious visions occurred and the believer was astonished. He was worried about the visions that occurred to him several times and eventually he prayed, asking God to take back the gift. Surprisingly, no more visions occurred to him.

God foretells things that will happen to you through visions. You may not figure out what the vision means. But the vision is a proof that the Holy Spirit is with you when you are praying. You do not have to be surprised but you should keep on praying. If your pastor is positive about this gift, then you should go and talk to him. However, there are pastors who are cautious about it.

Firstly, if you have seen a vision while praying, it is advisable not to inform the person who is related to the vision about what you have seen. This is true especially when the content of the vision is negative. Even if the content of the vision is positive, it is advisable to watch what will happen because it could be accomplished or might not be accomplished. Believe that God has shown you what will be accomplished and pray for the person who is related to your vision.

Secondly, if the Holy Spirit has worked within you through a vision, then you must also realise that evil spirits will try to show you a strange vision. You should always stay awake and pray in order not to be tempted. Evil spirits come to you and show fake visions when you feel angry, sad, or hate someone. The spiritual world is a battlefield, and according to your spiritual status, there can either be the work of the Holy Spirit or of evil spirits. Leave your pride behind, your thinking that only you can see the work and vision of the Holy Spirit. That is why people with the gift of the Holy Spirit have to humble themselves.

Thirdly, people with the gifts of prophecy and visions have to speak few words. Unconsciously, they will feel that they want to tell somebody about what they have seen, heard and experienced. But that is a temptation. Speaking about the spiritual world that you have experienced without hesitation is an act that breaks down church order. The church will be in confusion if you tell your fellow believers about what you saw and heard through visions and prophecy. This is because not all of the believers have those kinds of gifts. They may interpret your vision as a manifestation of your emotions.

Therefore, whatever you see, you must keep praying and watching. Speaking about a vision before it is achieved will not only bring confusion to your church, but also make you look ridiculous. It is not a wise measure to take. Even after your vision or prophecy has been achieved, try not to be boastful about it so you can keep yourself away from evil spirits.

Fourthly, visions can or cannot be seen. It is a gift of the Holy Spirit and it belongs to Him. Do not try too hard to see something. Do not think that you have not received any grace because you have not seen something on a particular day. Just follow the Holy Spirit and pray hard. You do not need to be obsessed with an idea that you have to see something. You will see something only if the Spirit wants you to see it. A flexible mind is required to follow the Holy Spirit. Do not regard yourself as a special person and show off because you hear something when you pray. In other words do not become arrogant, for evil spirits have a special liking for arrogant people.

Fifthly, never forget that the Word of God is the most important thing in the world. If you have received the gift of visions, you have to stay as close to the Bible, the Word of God, as possible. All gifts have to be interpreted with the Word of God. Therefore, you must read and meditate on the Bible and wash your eyes and ears before you pray. If not, your contaminated eyes and ears may distort the vision given by the Holy Spirit.

Gift of healing

All of us want to be free from illnesses and live a healthy life. But in reality, we get sick, or our children or our neighbors suffer from illnesses. Every time we encounter such problems we feel pain. God is a healer who heals us (Ex. 15:26). His Son Jesus also healed people throughout His life (Mt. 12:15). Jesus gave the power to heal to his disciples (Lk. 9:1). Paul said the power to heal is a gift of the Holy Spirit (1 Co. 12:9). The gift of healing is perhaps the most practical gift. When our children have fever we usually lay our hands on them and pray, expecting God to heal them.

What happened that night?

When I was in the third year of high school, which was the time to study hard for the university entrance examination, I caught an unknown illness. My head would get hot and catch fever whenever I tried to study. I had to put my head on a wall during every break at school in order to cool it down. I just could not study even for a minute. And it was summer vacation. My mother decided to take me to a doctor. We asked around and found a neuropsychiatric doctor in Gunsan Jeollabukdo. When we were going there by bus, I thought we should pray to God before we reached the clinic. So we stopped by Deokam Church in Changhang. Minister Moon was the pastor there and she was the one who was praying and sharing life together with my mother.

Minister Moon was a woman minister in her mid 30s. She was really faithful to God. She read the Bible day and night and fasted and prayed all the time. I felt some kind of a mysterious atmosphere when I first met her. After hearing from my mother, Minister Moon prayed for me.

She prayed in tongues first and interpreted whatever she uttered every time she prayed. She told me that this illness had no name, that it could not be cured and that no one could fix it. She also said that God would heal my illness within three days and show His power. Also, she said that I should go to a church and pray in the evening for three days so that the Holy Spirit could come and work with power to heal my illness.

Her prophecy was so surprising. However, my mother and I continued our journey to the hospital. I talked to a doctor and then I was laid on a bed with so many wires and detectors on my head. My mother could not stop crying. After several hours of examination, the doctor came to me.

"This is an incurable disease with no name. I think stress is the cause…because you are preparing for a national examination. I suggest you stop your study and take a good rest."

And he gave me a prescription and told me to relax and stay in a stable condition. I was struck with dismay. I could not accept the doctor's prescription that easily. I was in my third year of high school and I had to study. But I had no recourse but to take the prescription and come back home. I had to believe what minister Moon had said. I made up my mind to pray hard for three days from that day.

I started to pray at 9 o'clock that night at a church. My prayer was just a mumbling because I had not received the power of prayer. I prayed while thinking, 'She said the Holy Spirit will work powerfully!' However, my prayer on the first day was not that good. I was just mumbling and that was

Seeking gifts of the Holy Spirit

it. I was a little bit disappointed. But there was nothing else I could do except for praying.

Then I waited for the second night. At 9 o'clock, I went to church and started praying. I was still a beginner in praying but that day I felt some kind of strength supporting my prayer. There was a sister whom I knew well, praying 8 meters away from me. And a really strange thing happened. Her prayer was set on fire. And I sensed that she was praying very hard for me. There was no reason for her to pray for me, but she was giving a strong intercession through the Holy Spirit. She was praying on behalf of me. I really had to pray harder than her. After the prayer she came over to me.

"Today is strange. God wanted me to pray only for you, Sung-min!"

It was hot summer and she was soaked with sweat all over because of her ardent prayer. I was really grateful to her.

It was the last day of my prayer. I was expecting something to happen. It was Friday. Our church was having an all-night prayer meeting, and at least 20 students, youth and adults, were present. The night prayer meeting started and each and every one felt something was different while they prayed. They were praying in the powerful presence of the Holy Spirit. I was swept away by the atmosphere and I was crying out loud, although I could not pray in tongues.

I was shouting out my prayer like that for a while and suddenly someone shouted at me, "Sung-min! Pray harder!" What was that? It was a familiar voice. It was the voice of the vice president of the student council. Unlike myself, who had not received tongues and avoided prayer meetings, everyone was on fire while they prayed. I think she was praying with her spiritual eyes opened. She kept on praying in a loud voice, "Sung-min! Cry out!" I said to myself, "The Holy Spirit is working through her today!" I was also convinced that God was with me and that my illness would be cured. On the next morning, I realised that my head was clear. I was completely healed. It was through this incident that I experienced the power of the Holy Spirit.

Why do some people do not get healed?

I put my full trust in the gift of healing after experiencing the power of the Holy Spirit. But the problem was that I also started to lay my hands on ailing believers and pray for them, although I did not have the power to heal. As a result, I witnessed so many strange episodes during the twenty years of my ministry.

This is a story of a famous pastor in his early time of ministry. A believer brought a sick chick to him and requested him to pray. Holding the neck of the chick, the pastor ardently prayed. When he finished his prayer and opened his eyes, he saw a dead chick with its eyes popped out.

When I was studying in America, I served as an education minister at a New York church. I was in my early 20s and was responsible for instructing middle and high school students. One day, my wife and I and Mr. Lee and his wife, who were instructing the students, went for a picnic. Soon after we arrived at the picnic spot, Mr. Lee suffered a stomach ache. I thought our prayer could heal the pain, so my wife and I and Mr. Lee's wife started to pray together for him. However, nothing happened. He begged us to go home, but holding his arms, I prayed several times more. I had a feeling that because of my faith God would make him feel better. Mr. Lee was such a good person: He endured the simple but foolish faith of a naïve minister and received our prayers.

Why did he not get better despite my prayers? Maybe it was because I had faith that God would heal him, but I lacked the power to heal. The power of healing the sick belongs to God. But the power of God works through people of faith. Therefore, I think, receiving the power or gift of healing is very critical to the ministry of healing.

Power to heal

The power to heal is a gift of the Holy Spirit. The Holy Spirit can give us the gift of healing when we are in the fullness of the Spirit. Our church has specialised in healing headaches. I think God gave me such a gift. Those who come to church with aching heads feel better when I pray with them. Sometimes people with shoulder pain come and, while they pray, their pains go away. The major gift of healing given to me was the power to heal headaches. That is why our church people say that this power is mysterious.

In 2000, I was in Brazil serving as an assistant pastor at a Korean church. The adults of our church gathered every Friday night for a prayer meeting. One night, a young minister named Marcion, who seemed to be about thirty years old, came to attend our prayer meeting. He was a minister who often fasted and went to the mountains to pray. He also read the Bible a lot and tried to live in accordance with the Scriptures. He was filled with the Holy Spirit and had many kinds of gifts. One of the gifts was the gift of healing.

Two to three believers with light illnesses like arthritis got healed through Marcion on the first day of the prayer meeting. My wife had a cyst and was feeling pain in her lower stomach. No one knew about it except me and my wife. At that time, Marcion did not know who my wife was and what part of her body was in pain. But he pointed out the part where the cyst was and said, "God's healing hand is working now in this part." Right at that moment my wife got cured! My wife told me about it later.

"For the first time in my life I felt something like a sharp and refreshing ray of light going through me like the spring!"

A deaconess who heard about him came to our next prayer meeting and got healed. Later the deaconess told me that she had been freed from chronic hemorrhoids. God cured the deaconess because she truly believed in the glory of God while she prayed.

How should we deal with the gift of divine healing?
Firstly, we should not blindly believe in the gift of healing.

What would you do if you have cancer? Would you choose to undergo an operation or get healed through the gift of healing? That is the question. You will have to seriously pray to resolve this problem.

God does heal our illnesses. But it is unwise to pray only seeking for miracles while disregarding modern medicine. If modern medicine has given up on you, then of course, you should find stability in a prayer meeting and yearn for the gift of healing. But when doctors suggest an operation, it will become a huge temptation for those who have good faith because in their heart they have faith that God will heal them.

All family members should pray together for the patient in this case. They should ask God to show them His plans. It would be better to consult an experienced pastor.

Secondly, we should not believe in modern medicine blindly. People who ignore the gift of healing and have faith only in modern medicine present a bigger problem. They only go for an operation. They ignore inspirations coming from God. We must realise how dangerous and unstable medical science can be. There are many wrong diagnoses and countless cases of people dying because of doctors' mistakes. We should first put our trust in God. Medicine comes next. But in a timely order, we should first go see a doctor for diagnosis. According to my experience, I think it is better to go to a large hospital at least three times to be examined for a critical disease so that we can avoid a wrong diagnosis. Then we have to choose whether we should undergo an operation after analysing the diagnoses or get cured through prayer. We need to make the wisest choice while relying on God.

A young sister, who was responsible for arranging flowers in our church, found it extremely hard to keep standing for a long time. So she went to see a famous doctor in Seoul. The doctor said that she needed to undergo surgery because she had a big cyst in her womb. She was going to get married soon and what the doctor said to her was a great shock to her. She came to see me under great pressure. She had cried so much that her face was all swollen. While I was praying I had a feeling that she should not hurry the surgery. So I sent her to see a gynecologist whom I knew well. The doctor said that it was true that she had a big cyst. But he suggested watching it for a while and then going for an ultrasound scan after two months. She had to make a decision. Should I undergo an operation? Or should I pray and wait? At last she chose to take my advice. Then she got married. After a year she called me.

"Pastor! I had a daughter. I owe you much for my baby."

Do not disregard inspiration coming from God while you are praying. You should pray before you go to a hospital. Do not hurry to undergo surgery after the doctor's diagnosis. Pray earnestly so that you end up taking the right steps.

Thirdly, you have to go along with modern medicine. The power of healing is very valuable to us. We can not think of not saying 'thank you' to a person who has cured a patient. However, there can be a serious problem if you depend too much on the gift of divine healing and ignore medicine. God also uses doctors and medicines to heal us.

Some parents decide to go for healing through prayer when their children contract diseases like tuberculosis or tympanitis—diseases that can be easily cured by taking antibiotics. Another person delayed undergoing surgery on his toe, attending prayer meetings. As a result, he had to get his leg amputated below his knee because of complications caused by diabetes. No matter how much you believe in God's power of healing, your faith is blind if you disregard medicine and surgery. We should avail ourselves of ultrasound, MRI or CT if required. But we must keep praying to God for quick recovery while being treated for our ailment: "God! Please let me encounter a good hospital today. Please let me meet a good doctor..."

Fourthly, you should take Western medicine for natural diseases. How can we help a person who suffers from headaches because of lack of adequate sleep? We should first pray for the person, because prayer always comes first. We should also tell the person to get enough sleep, as good sleep would help him or her in getting rid of the headache naturally.

How can we take care of a person suffering from common cold? You should pray for the person and tell him or her to get the right medicine. This person caught a cold because of his or her mistake, and since common cold is a natural disease, it can be easily cured by medicine. Common cold can also be cured through prayer. It is therefore advisable to combine prayer and medicine. A pastor should thus have full knowledge of the sick person's ailment before he starts praying for him or her. This requires discernment. Sometimes we can get an easy prescription when we know the cause.

Fifthly, illnesses caused by evil spirits have to be defeated through prayer. Evil spirits can break into our body and cause illness if our spiritual condition is bad. The symptoms can range from headache to diarrhea, shoulder pain, etc. No medicine is of use in such cases. Spiritual power is the only solution. We have to pray to cast out the evil spirits that make us suffer. That is the only way to cure the illness.

Spiritual penetration into the material world is invisible and we cannot tell for sure whether evil spirits are present or not. But if we are spiritually awake, we would be able to sense spiritual disorder and soon wage a spiritual war on evil spirits. When a pastor visits the home of a sick believer and goes back home, sometimes the symptoms shown by the believer appear on the pastor. A young minister may wonder why he is sick, but as he grows in experience he gets to know spiritual secrets. He learns that he has to defeat the evil spirits that infiltrate him after he visits a sick believer. Evil spirits lose their strength when their identity is exposed.

My Life and My Confession

God, My Healer

(Director, Barnabas Training Institute, and former Professor, Seoul Theological Seminary)

In 1988, I was hospitalised because of low weight and low blood pressure. And then for seven months, I attended a prayer meeting in Cheon-an to recuperate. While I was reading the book of Luke at the prayer my eyes were fixed on the part that said that Jesus fasted for 40 days, that He was tempted by the devil, that He won the spiritual war and that He went to Galilee led by the Holy Spirit. In the power of the Holy Spirit, Jesus went to Galilee to start His ministry. Isaiah's prophecy of the presence of the Holy Spirit was achieved through Jesus. Jesus cast out demons, opened the eyes of the blind and freed the prisoners. Earlier, I thought Jesus could do these things because he is God. But when I read the verse,

"He returned to Galilee in the power of the Holy Spirit," I realised that. Jesus could perform miracles not because he was God, but because He worked in the power of the Spirit. Jesus did Holy Spirit ministry.

I wrote the words "to Galilee in the power of the Spirit" in big letters on the wall of my room and started to pray. I had to recover in order to go to Galilee in the power of the Holy Spirit. For this, I prayed night and day. I prayed to God to send me to Galilee and to change my ministry to the ministry of the Holy Spirit, which was completely different from what I used to do before. In March, a friend of mine, who was a pastor ministering at Daejon, came to see me. When he saw me he cried out loud saying, "How can you stay in this bad environment for your recovery? A healthy man would surely return to illness here!" He was right. The room where I was staying did not get any sunlight. Also, people were burning dead leaves in the hall in front of my room, and smoke and dust came into my room. "I'll take you to a brighter prayer meeting. You just follow me," said my friend. I had to follow him without any excuse. The place he led me to was 'Galilee Prayer Mountain.' It was not Galilee in Israel. God took me to another Galilee and made me experience the ministry of the Holy Spirit.

Before I could experience spiritual power, God made me repent. Now I weigh 57 kg, but back then I weighed just 47 kg. "Until when will you leave me like this?" This was my prayer, and to my prayer the Holy Spirit asked me,

"Do you believe in divine healing?"
"I never denied it, God."
"I didn't ask that. I asked, do you believe."

I was about to say, "I do believe," but strangely all I could utter was "I do…" Suddenly, memories of my ministry came flooding in. I thought about my faith in divine healing. That happened when I was ministering in a church at Milyang after resigning from my position as a Professor at a seminary. There were many ill people among the church members. And they asked me, their pastor, to lay my hands on them to pray. I laid my hands on them, but could not ask them if their illness had been cured. It was because I was not confident. That gave me the belief that "they weren't healed although I prayed." I was compelled to give prayer, but I was not confident.

But God challenged my faith. So I repented and prayed to God to help me strengthen my faith. One day a young son of our minister caught a fever. His father was about to take him to hospital. But the boy said, "Dad! Why don't we go to Pastor Lee and ask him to pray for me?" So they came to me and I recalled how Jesus rebuked the fever of Peter's mother-in-law. I did the same as Jesus did. I rebuked the fever and prayed. After my prayer, the boy took a deep breath and said, "Wow! Now I'm okay!" and went out to play. The fever left him the moment I prayed. His little sister came and she also got healed. Her friend came the next day to receive prayer and he also got cured. Four children had the same fever and they all got healed. From that time on the news spread that I was a healing minister.

After that, adults started to come. A sister in her 30s, who had been converted through our evangelisation, had a problem in her kidney. Her face was also swollen all over. She came to me for prayer, but when I was about to pray for her my faith suddenly dipped. I doubted if my prayer would work for adults, although it had worked well for children. My hand would not go up. So I told her to come back after four days. I told her to pray while she waited. Then I started to pray, asking for simple faith. Four days later she came and received my prayer and got healed.

Another sister, who was in her 40s, came. She had hemorrhoids. My hand would not go up again, so I told her to come back a few days later and pray while she waited. We prayed for three days in preparation. She came and I prayed for her. Blood and pus fell down from her and the hemorrhoids dried up. God was training me to work as a healing minister.

At the end of July of the same year, I came out of the prayer meeting and applied for the post of Professor at Seoul Theological University. At the school, I volunteered to be Director of the dormitory because I wanted to do Holy Spirit ministry. That position was wanted by no one. But I wanted to do a ministry led by the Holy Spirit every morning. One day the dean of the school came to me and asked me to lay my hands on him. He was my professor when I was a student. Anyway, I laid my hands on him. He had a ruptured disc in his back. I prayed laying my hands on his back, and his disc was healed. Another student came before the early morning service started. The student said he could not sleep because he was sick. So I prayed for him, and his illness was gone.

One day I prayed and asked the Holy Spirit to let the students experience power through my sermon at the school chapel. I preached to one thousand students and felt as if they were being sucked into the sermon. After the service, one graduate school student came to my office. "Professor, I had terribly bad eyesight and I couldn't see the black board. But today when I was listening to your sermon, faith took over. Now I believe that God will heal my sight," said the student and asked for my prayer. He then took off his glasses. Afterwards, the Holy Spirit continued to work through my preaching ministry. At first, many people got healed while listening to sermons. I thanked God for His presence in the Spirit at the scenes of the sermons.

I was leading a revival meeting at Yeonmu Central Methodist Church. Several people got healed during the revival meeting. One deaconess bought me dinner and told me that she had been ill for six years from a ruptured disc in her neck and that she had to pay so much money for oriental medicine, western medicine and massage treatment, but none could do anything for her. She said she was healed when her body was heated up while listening to my preaching.

The Evangelism Explosion team of Seoul Theological University came to Jeonwon Church located near Chungbuk University in Cheongju. They came to evangelise the university. Professors and students came and spread gospel message and, after their ministry, had a conference. I went to the conference to preach. On the second day, I was eating a slice of watermelon with their pastor. Someone knocked on the door. He used to be partially deaf before, but he said he felt the volume of the microphone going up while I was preaching. It was his ear getting healed! Quite a few people were healed during the sermon. Through this experience I pray to receive the message of God and for the work of the Holy Spirit every time I prepare sermons. When I preach, I preach with the belief that the work of the Spirit will be done.

I run a training center called Barnabas Training Institute in Okcheon, Chungbuk. Hundreds of pastors and their wives come to the Institute every year for spiritual training. One part of the training is the gift of healing. Many pastors and their wives experienced healing during lectures and praise time. Even after returning to their church, they experienced the glory of God the healer.

Chapter 7

Bearing the fruit of the Holy Spirit

The gifts of the Holy Spirit are given to us to make our religious life more vibrant. They are given to us according to our character and individuality. Some people receive the gift of tongues, while others receive the gift of spreading the message of Christ. Some people receive the gift of healing, while others receive the gift of leadership. Some people receive the gift of prophecy, while others receive the gift of service. Although the gifts of the Holy Spirit enrich our religious life, their absence does not hinder our religious life in any way.

To make it clear, the gifts of the Holy Spirit have no relation to our being saved. We have to believe in Jesus Christ in order to be saved from our sins and become children of God. Therefore, the gifts of the Holy Spirit are only to help those who are saved by believing in Jesus and to help them live a good Christian life. This does not mean that we can ignore the gifts of the Holy Spirit. I just want to make it clear that the gifts of the Holy Spirit cannot guarantee our salvation.

Also, if a person, who has received a gift of the Holy Spirit, becomes arrogant, there is a high possibility that evil spirits would use him or her as their weapon. We can manipulate the gifts of the Spirit. We might also sell the grace of God by asking for money in return for a healing. That is not correct.

In conclusion, we cannot tell whether a Christian's faith is mature or not by a gift of the Spirit. The standard to determine the maturity should be based on the fruit of the Holy Spirit. We sometimes see that there are people who received gifts of tongues and prophecy from God and yet their personalities are stiff and harsh. We get disappointed with them when they set bad examples. And sometimes we feel we cannot trust the gifts of the Holy Spirit. In fact, there are several cases of people with gifts of prophecy or divine healing causing trouble in churches because of lack of religious maturity.

Here is a pertinent question: How should we deal with the gifts of the Holy Spirit?

The gifts of the Holy Spirit have to continue to bear the fruits of the Holy Spirit. The fruits of the Holy Spirit, which are very closely connected to the maturity of Christian faith, are the standard to determine whether our faith is real or not. Therefore, we must try our best to develop the gifts of the Holy Spirit into the fruits of the Holy Spirit. If we do this, the revival of the church would be evident.

We must have the fruit of the Holy Spirit

We can say that the gifts of the Holy Spirit are an option; we may or may not receive them. But on the other hand, the fruit of the Holy Spirit is not an option; we must have it. It is written in the book of Galatians chapter 5, verse 22, "But the fruit of the Spirit is love, joy, peace, patience, kindness, goodness, faithfulness, gentleness and self-control. Against such things there is no law." Through this passage we can learn that there are nine kinds of fruit of the Holy Spirit. But before we go ahead we must know that in the passage the word 'fruit' is not in the plural form but in the singular. We can interpret this as those nine kinds of fruits that are not produced separate to each other but in integration and almost simultaneously.

Now, let us look at these nine fruits of the Holy Spirit.

Among these nine fruits of the Holy Spirit, love is what God has ordered us to have (Deut. 6:5, Mt. 22:337-40). The fruit of love is the representative fruit of the Holy Spirit. Paul described love in 1Corinthians chapter 13 as follows. "Love is patient, love is kind. It does not envy, it does not boast, it is not proud. It is not rude, it is not self-seeking, it is not easily angered, it keeps no record of wrongs. Love does not delight in evil but rejoices in the truth. It always protects, always trusts, always hopes, and always perseveres. Love never fails. But where there are prophecies, the prophecies will cease; where there are tongues, the tongues will be stilled."

We can see that the characteristics of love depicted in 1Co. 13 are almost similar to that of the fruit of the Holy Spirit. Yes, love is the core of the fruit of the Holy Spirit. People who receive the gift of the Holy Spirit have to pursue the fruit and gift of love. We can become the most ideal Christians if we use the gifts of the Holy Spirit with our love toward God and our neighbors. God is love (1Jn. 4:7-8). Jesus is the fruit of God's love (1Jn. 4:9-10). Christians are disciples who follow after the life of Jesus. Therefore Christians have to love God and their neighbors 1Jn 4:11-12).

Love, the biggest gift

"Love never fails. But where there are prophecies, the prophecies will cease; where there are tongues, the tongues will be stilled; where there is knowledge, it will pass away."(1Co. 13:8).

The gifts of the Holy Spirit have been given to us to fulfill our temporary needs. However, we need love not only when we are on this earth, but also when we are in heaven. Love is our right and responsibility. "And over all these virtues put on love" says the book of Colossus. We have to put on the fruit of love upon all the gifts we have received.

However, it is not an easy thing to love God and our neighbors. It seems the fruit of love is too far to reach. It may be easy to become a Christian with power, full of gifts and full of words. But it is hard to become a Christian whose heart is filled with love.

How can we bear the fruit of love? We cannot achieve the order of love, fruit of love and gift of love in our own strength. We can only obey this order through the Holy Spirit. We can only live with love when the Holy Spirit abides in us and rules and leads us (1Jn. 4:13). We can never forgive or love our enemies with our own brevity. We must be in the fullness of the Holy Spirit in order to bear the fruit of love.

We naturally bear the fruit of love if we are in the Holy Spirit (Jn. 5:4-5). It means that we are not in the Spirit if we have not borne the fruit of love (Jn. 15:6). Love is the fruit that Christians should bear. But most of the Christians give up the fruit of love saying that it is difficult to keep. I see love as the fruit of the Holy Spirit and the gift of the Holy Spirit. If love is the gift of the Spirit, we should ask for it. The gift of healing and gift of prophecy are indeed important, but the gift of love is of more importance. This is because through the fruit of love we can bear the other eight fruits of the Holy Spirit and prove that we are true Christians.

We can seek various gifts. But most of all, we should seek the gift of love. Just imagine how good it will be when the gift of love continues to grow into the fruit of love and fruit of the Holy Spirit! When I was serving in a Korean church in Brazil, a person, who used to be a Buddhist, became a Christian through radical conversion.

I assume most of the people know that when Buddhists become Christians they become truly loyal to Jesus. They are different from others when they come for early morning service. They arrive 30 minutes before the service. They take a shower to clean themselves before they come to church. I feel ashamed when I compare myself to them. When I was a minister I used to arrive at church 10 minutes before the service and would not even wash my face properly before leaving for church. And many a time I failed to notice that my tie was a bit crushed.

This newly-converted Christian came for early morning service with special zeal. But he had one problem: He hated his nagging wife. Sometimes he even felt like killing her.

One early morning, the Holy Spirit said to him: "Love your wife!" It was a strange voice that he heard for the first time in his life and it really electrified him. Then he went back home from church and saw his wife, who was fast asleep. Strangely, he felt compassion for her. After that experience he repented for ill-treating his wife. He started developing a strong liking for her, which soon grew into love. When his wife noticed the change in him she truly started to love him.

Love makes our life easy. We are the children of God and yet we hate so many people. Some say the Holy Spirit cannot do anything about the tension that normally characterises the relationship between a woman and her daughter-in-law. There are problems between brothers, church members, fathers and sons. Truly, there are so many people that we need to forgive. But we usually end up hating them because of our narrow-mindedness.

Let us together receive the gift of love. Let us pray to God, and the Holy Spirit will give us gifts of faith and love! This is why Paul advised us to long for love more than any other gift (1Co. 13:1-3).

Weapons for spiritual war

The fruit of the Holy Spirit can be regarded as a process of being sanctified. We can bear the fruit of the Holy Spirit only after defeating evil spirits. Evil spirits lose their power as we bear more fruits of the Holy Spirit. Gentle and modest persons have few tests to take. But there are many works of evil spirits for those who are self-centered and have no love. Therefore, the fruit of the Holy Spirit is the most effective and powerful weapon for fighting the spiritual war against evil spirits.

One Christian woman lives in agony, as she fights so often with her husband. And she says she just cannot figure out why there are so many evil spirits working on her. In this case, evil sprits can work freely mainly because the woman has a sharp and hard personality.

This personality trait can be found in many Christian ministers. The number of tests will grow less as our personality develops. People normally tend not to admit that they are the problem in their relationship with others due to their defective personality. They attribute the problem to external factors, such as evil spirits. Still, it is true that evil spirits grip us when we lose control of our emotions.

Also, evil spirits use our weakness to embroil us in disputes with other people. It is our imperfect personality—not the work of evil spirits—that prevents us from defeating the evil forces operating within us. In order to win the spiritual war against evil spirits, we must bear the fruit of the Holy Spirit.

Thus, people with a sanguine temperament should try to bear the fruit of patience; bilious people should try to bear the fruit of control; melancholic people should try to bear the fruit of joy; phlegmatic people should bear the fruit of faithfulness.

Imagine how convenient our life would be if we could bring our enemies to our side! We can do so through love. Romans 12:20 says we should give bread and drink to the enemy for revenge! This is a paradoxical expression that shows the power of love. A Korean proverb says: Give a piece of bread to the one you hate. This means that people of other faith also understand the true worth of love. It is love that enables us to defeat evil spirits.

Chapter 8
In the front line of spiritual war

When I was attending a service at a revival center, I saw a woman spinning around a handkerchief in the air. At first I thought it was God's grace that made her perform that strange act. But when she started moving towards the pulpit, I immediately noticed that she was possessed by a demon. "Look at that crazy woman! Look at that crazy woman!" someone shouted. The speaker of the service had a perplexed look on his face. Eventually, staff members took her away.

Some mentally deranged people look almost normal; we may mistake them for normal people. Such people live in their own world, have auditory hallucinations, see visions and try to relate their experience to the real world. Also, they are unable to have normal relationships with people around them. Such people cause their family members a lot of grief.

People possessed by evil spirits

Evil spirits usually go into a person who experiences unbearable shock or sudden fear. This is why we have to be careful when we pray alone in remote places, such as mountains, caves and valleys. It is especially dangerous to pray at night. Many people are caught by evil spirits when they pray alone in the mountains. Demons invade when people feel sudden fear and terror while praying alone in the dark.

Joseph Smith (1805-1844), the head of Mormonism, seriously thought about which church is the true church. While he was thinking about it he meditated on the verse, "But when he asks, he must believe and not doubt" (Jm. 1:6). Then he went into a wood to ask God which church is the true one. While he was praying alone something in a black form suddenly overpowered him. He rolled on the ground groaning with pain. Then he saw and heard a vision and had auditory hallucination. He saw a second vision on September 23, 1823, when he was praying at his bed. He met Moronai, whom he thought was the messenger of God, and received a revelation. From that night until the next day he saw four visions and found a golden plate in Hill Cumorah. That golden plate is the Mormon Bible.

By analysing what Joseph Smith had experienced, we can learn that he was possessed by an evil spirit when he was praying alone in the woods. Praying alone in the woods at an early age was the cause of being possessed by the evil spirit. An evil spirit, which was beside him, entered him when he was frightened while praying. Now that he was possessed by the evil spirit he could not avoid all the visions and hallucinations that the evil spirit was giving him. The messenger of God he met, of course, was a demon. Joseph Smith thought he received a revelation from God, and the angel he met was a messenger of God. Unfortunately, he was used by an evil spirit.

These kinds of tricks of the evil spirits are hidden behind all heresy sects. Most of the leaders of the sects believe that they have received revelations from God, but actually they are cheated by demons' clever trickery. This is why Paul said that Satan also masquerades as an angel of light (2Co. 11:14).

We can be easily possessed by evil spirits in our daily lives. Evil spirits invade us when parents are abusing and committing violence on their children, when a husband is beating his wife, when a younger brother, who is being beaten by his older brother, is extremely frightened and so on. We often say that people who do these things are insane. If people who have been abused or beaten do not get insane, they are, at the very least, deeply hurt inside. Evil spirits come in and go out through the wound at all times. Those who grow up being abused and beaten up develop a cantankerous character. Such people are quick to anger and lead a turbulent married life. They also ill-treat their children. Such people often regret their actions after calming down. But they do not take long to fall into a similar situation again. They do not act according to their senses and cannot control their emotions, no matter how much they suffer. This is because evil spirits are coming into them through their hidden wounds at all times. When their wounds are touched, evil spirits come and take control of them. Such people may not be insane, but it is obvious that they are possessed by something. This is how abuse and violence, which destroy a family, continue to flow onto the next generation. Evil spirits can cause a great deal of mischief in our lives.

Oh, my stalker!
I was serving as an assistant minister in 2000 at a Korean church in Brazil. One of the people whom I remember the most was brother Byoung-su. He was in his late twenties and he used to wander around Sao Paulo downtown in his bare feet all night long. However, very strangely, he always came to our Wednesday and Friday late-night prayer meetings exactly on time. He used to stare at me whenever I preached. Sometimes he sat with vacant eyes. He looked more like a stalker to me. He never spoke a word to me, but keenly

observed me. That was really a burden to me. No one knew what to do about him. We could not send him out nor could we welcome him to our evening services and prayer meetings. What I learned through him was that we cannot do anything about people who are possessed by an evil spirit. My inability to do anything about it drove me to despair.

Secrets of the spiritual world

One day, in a late night prayer meeting, someone who just got converted to Christianity came. Byoung-su also came that night as usual and, in that troubled atmosphere, the prayer meeting began. We prayed in a circle. The new believer suddenly started perspiring profusely and lay down on the floor. He did not get up during the prayer meeting. Everyone wondered what had happened. But I knew what was going on. The new believer was spiritually weak and could not resist Byoung-su's spiritual influence. So we started to sing praise and pray even harder. Sensing the ongoing spiritual war, I passionately clapped my hands and prayed really hard.

The next week, our choir conductor came to the prayer meeting. He said that his waist started to hurt when Byoung-su came into the church. I noticed that the evil spirit attacked only those who were spiritually weak. Church members, who learned about this strange phenomenon, struggled hard to be on their guard against attacks by evil spirits. We put Byoung-su in between me and my wife because people were so afraid of him. The situation got a little better. Yes, my wife and I were a little bit stronger spiritually than the others. But I did not have the power to control and drive out the demon in him. I learned then about my spiritual limit.

Then one day, the deaconess from another church, who had spiritual power, came to attend our prayer meeting upon our invitation. They were a prayer group from Sao Paulo

United Presbyterian Church. That night they, instead of us, fought the spiritual war with Byoung-su. They attempted to cast out the demon in the name of Jesus Christ many times. But nothing happened until the prayer meeting was finished. They got exhausted and went back home. Later I heard that they all got sick and had to stay in bed after the night of the spiritual war.

One of the deaconesses who came to our prayer meeting took me to a revival meeting. The revival meeting was lead by a pastor's wife from a Korean church in America. She was full of the Holy Spirit, had gifts of prophecy and was casting out evil spirits. But when she looked at Byoung-su she said, "I'd have to give up this revival meeting if I should heal this person." And then she just continued the meeting for the other people. She gave up at the first sight of him. She had penetrated his spiritual condition right away. This is why the deaconesses suffered from illness—because they did not know about it.

Develop your spiritual power

One of our church members called for Marcion, who was a Brazilian minister. He had a bright look on his face because he did a lot of fasting and prayers in the mountains. It seemed that Byoung-su was feeling somewhat controlled when Marcion showed up. We were all expecting a showdown between Marcion and Byoung-su. Will the evil spirit leave Byoung-su? Holding our breath, we watched every move Marcion made. Byoung-su sat still when Marcion went closer to him. And when Marcion laid his hand on Byouns-su's head, he feebly dropped his head down. It was like a mouse before a cat. It was not like the Byoung-su we used to see. Then I said to myself, "There are different classes in spiritual world!" Marcion prayed for a while for Byoung-su. And then he said to me and our church members. "He is a person that

God has specially sent for you. You have to pray hard to drive out the demon from him." I was crying inside when I heard that. "Oh! My God! Does that mean I have to cast it out?" From then on I regarded praying hard as my mission and duty.

We could not cast the evil spirit out from Byoung-su that night. But we noticed that Byoung-su, who used to cause uproars, was so calm and quiet. He used to clap and sing praise with a strange look in prayer meetings and stare at each believer. Also, whenever we prayed in tongues, he prayed with his hands shaking up and down violently as if he were opposing us. But it was different that day. I then determined that I should develop my spiritual power and authority. That day I concluded that I had to win the spiritual war against evil spirits by having a large sword of the Holy Spirit.

Fight against an evil spirit

From then on I waited for the Friday prayer meeting to come. I eagerly looked forward to fighting against the evil spirit that was working through Byoung-su. Obviously, I was filled with power. The spiritual war continued in great tension for several months. I was spiritually confident. Byoung-su was the one who showed the best attendance and spiritual enthusiasm. He showed up at the exact time without fail and observed us and disturbed our service. Through him I clearly learned about the reality of the evil spirit, which was not visible to our eyes. God showed me the reality of the spiritual world through Byoung-su. There is a Christian who does his best to speak the Gospel. But there is always a demon who is zealous to disturb the Gospel of Jesus.

One day, when we were praying in the fullness of the Holy Spirit, Byoung-su was also praying hard in the fullness of something. When the prayer reached its peak, Byoung-su started to swing his arms up and down with great passion. Not knowing myself, I reached him and stood in front of him. While others were praying where they were, only I was the one who stood face to face with him. What I did was something I could not have done before. At first I was brave enough to stand, but when I looked straight into his eyes I almost fainted. And then I regretted, saying "We should have prayed all together to drive out the evil spirit...Why am I doing this so foolishly?" But it was too late. I had to directly face the evil spirit that was working inside Byoung-su. But that day he also prayed harder than any other day and his eyes looked different. But it was not strong enough to overwhelm me. And at the same time I felt that my spiritual power was also not strong enough to face him. Yet, I bravely shouted at him, watching his eyes.

"In the name of Jesus of Nazareth, I order you, demon, to get out of this beloved son now!"

Byoung-su got mad and turned his head to his side and went out of the church. When I looked at his back while he was going out, I felt something was missing. That is how the prayer meeting that night ended.

Strange things happened afterwards

Strange things happened after Byoung-su went back. The next Monday afternoon, I started the engine of a church van, as I had to pick up my children at school. I put the van in reverse gear to take it out of the garage. But, unconsciously, I pressed the accelerator rather hard, and the van suddenly swooshed back 10 meters from the garage. It happened in the blink of an eye and I was too bewildered. So were my wife and our Brazilian neighbors. Accidentally, I bumped hard into a car that was parked across the street. Until then I was a safe driver; I had never had an accident before. I just could not understand why I drove like that. Our church had to pay for the insurance to fix the cars.

A strange and awkward week went like that and finally it was Friday night prayer meeting time. I encouraged myself to go to church. I determined to defeat the demon through hard prayer. But guess what happened? Most of the people who prayed together to stand against the evil spirit came with exhausted mind and body! At a glance I could notice how they had spent their rough week. Many of them were sick and in bed. Some of them had towels around their neck and were coughing. They all said in one voice, "Pastor! Please finish it fast today!"

It was sad that we could not fight properly once more. Moreover, Byoung-su was sitting defiantly with a sneer in his usual place. We sang praises but Byoung-su sang even more joyfully than us; and we really felt disheartened. It felt as if the evil spirit was celebrating its victory and laughing at us. At the same time, I regretted that this had happened because I spurred the demon on last week. That experience bolstered up my determination to remove the evil spirit from Byoung-su by strengthening the sword of the Holy Spirit.

Poor Byoung-su!
I pitied Byoung-su every time I saw him. So I bought him bread and some beverage at a café whenever I had a chance. But of course, personal conversation was nearly impossible. I tried to get closer to him personally, but it was not that easy. Actually, eating meals together at a café was unimaginable at first because I would not even dare to do so. However, as my spiritual confidence had grown considerably, I did not find it hard to have meals with him

His face had a dark tan and his hairline had started to recede. His bare feet were stained with dirt. One day, as I was walking down the street, I saw Byoung-su. I took him to our church. I asked questions about him. Although personal conversation was difficult, he answered some of my questions. He told me that his father and brother used to beat him often. One day his brother had lifted him up and thrown him down. I conjectured that the evil spirit must have gone into him on that occasion—when he felt fear. Since then he could not adapt himself to the society.

My wife asked him if he believed in Jesus. He answered, "I know Jesus." My wife told him that he should believe in Jesus, not just know about Him. Then she asked again if he believed in Jesus. But his answer remained the same, "I know who Jesus is."

Through Byoung-su, we confirmed that evil spirits know about Jesus but do not believe in Him. Evil spirits know well about Jesus and in order to have eternal life, they disturb those who have faith in Him. They tempt people of the world to fall into everlasting hell together with them.

I went back to America to finish my doctoral dissertation after one and a half years of ministry at a Korean church in Brazil. During my ministry in Brazil, although I could not free Byoung-su from the demon possession, I had experienced spiritual growth through Byoung-su. During those times, I not only learned about the secret of the spiritual world, but also armed myself spiritually.

My ministry in Brazil was almost over. Byoung-su usually remained very quiet during prayer meetings. When Marcion came and laid his hands on him to pray Byoung-su could not do anything but helplessly drop his head down. And before I knew it I was doing it too. When I approached him and laid my hands on his head, he helplessly dropped down his head and could not resist. My spiritual sword became very sharp during the spiritual war against the evil spirit that was working through Byoung-su. After I left for America, I heard that Byoung-su had returned to Korea.

How do we defeat evil spirits?

First, you need to have the sword of the Holy Spirit to defeat evil spirits. We can have the sword and the Word (Eph. 6:11-19) of the Holy Spirit with prayer. Jesus defeated Satan's temptation with the word of God. This is why it is so important to memorise and meditate on the Word. We have to engrave the Word of God on our heart and hold on to it and pray.

We cannot see the sword of the Holy Spirit with our eyes. But evil spirits can know the condition of our sword. If we have a powerful sword and good faith, then demon-possessed people become powerless in front of us, because demons within them notice our sword and hide from it. But if your sword is rusty and weak, they laugh at you and make a fool of you.

It is not hard to know the condition of our sword of the Holy Spirit. If you are a pastor, then it will be naturally revealed through the relationship that you have with your church members. If the pastor is armed with prayer and the Word and filled with the Holy Spirit, then all the believers will become like gentle sheep. But when believers become like goats and disobey and challenge the pastor, then the pastor has to check his spiritual status. To a pastor, obedience of believers is like a spiritual sensor.

How then can laymen know their spiritual condition? It is easy. Observe your children. If they are obedient and enthusiastic in church, then your spiritual status is okay. But if they are disobedient, defiant and wandering around, you have to repent your sins and sharpen your sword again. Your children will obey you if your sword of the Holy Spirit is sharp and powerful. We have to face the reality of the fierce spiritual war we are fighting. Our struggle is not against flesh and blood, but against the powers of the dark world and against the spiritual forces of evil in the heavenly realms (Eph. 6:12).

One of our church members' families had a spiritual sensor, and that was their second daughter. Whenever her parents' faith dropped, she experienced spiritual harassment at night. It seemed that an evil spirit came and pushed her down. She spoke gibberish and screamed and cried out loud. She was a smart and kind-hearted girl but occasionally stirred up her parents' heart. But before this happened, it was her parents' faith that had already dropped.

Her mom was a Buddhist before she became a Christian and she unconsciously uttered words such as "I miss temple food," and "Sometime I want to go to a temple because I used to go there with my mother when I was young" while praying at a prayer meeting. And her father uttered negative words such as, "Prayer time is rather long," "I'm tired in the morning because the prayer meeting finishes late," and "Why don't we go home and have a service."

Firstly, we should always check on our spiritual condition. We should find out whether or not we are lazy or disobedient to God's Word. If our sensor warns about our spiritual laziness, then we should immediately repent and come closer to God. An evil spirit could be a necessary evil because it makes us stay awake.

Secondly, we should protect ourselves from the devil's fire arrows with the shield of faith. Ordinary believers cannot defeat a person like Byoung-su, who is totally possessed by a demon. Spiritual experts and prayer warriors have to team up in order to stand against evil spirits to save those who are possessed by them. Therefore, we should rather prepare to fight the spiritual war that is close to us than focus on building up our strength to cast out all the demons in this world. It is more important to resist demonic attack with the shield of faith than to find out where evil spirits are and attack them.

We should protect ourselves and our families from an evil spirit's fire arrows with the shield of faith. Then we have to defend ourselves against forces of evil through our church. If you think that you are leading the battle of your church and take pride in yourself, then it means that you are already being used as a tool by an evil spirit. Never forget that modesty is the most powerful spiritual weapon.

Also, spiritual discernment is required to defeat evil spirits. We can easily identify an evil spirit residing in a person. But it is not easy to identify the evil spirits that roam freely, harassing and attacking people. When I as a pastor observe the believers, I see evil spirits wandering around, looking for an opportunity to attack them. When we pray for a Christian who has been possessed by an evil spirit and free him or her, the evil spirit enters another weak member of the congregation.

Our faith in God deepens when we fight against evil forces. But we must also consider the spiritual discernment of a pastor and believers. We will never lose the spiritual battle in our church if we know about spiritual flow, that is, where the evil spirit is going. Then the pastor's influence will be enlarged and the believers' growth will be accelerated. This may be the reason why Paul said that everything works for the good.

A pastor and his wife are likely to fight with each other after visiting a couple who has just had a fight, although they may be highly devoted to each other. They may not know why they are fighting at first, and their fight may turn into a so-called "bloody fight." When they get exhausted by the fight, they may realise that they have been deceived by an evil spirit. Sometimes they just cannot stop fighting, although they may know that the discord was engendered by the evil spirit. The couple needs to calm down and pray to God for harmony.

You also need to heal your wounded emotions to drive out the evil spirit. Many people, although they are normal, suffer on account of evil spirits. They fail to overcome their past wounds and sorrows and every night think about them. They are helpless, and the evil spirit comes in through the crack. They declare war against the evil spirit when they are spiritually fulfilled and are triumphant. But when their wounds are touched they stop fighting the spiritual war. Demons are well aware of our weak points; they touch them at all the time. A spouse or a fellow Christian might unintentionally say something, and an evil spirit suppresses the person through those words and makes the person disarm himself or herself. This is why we need to understand each other's wounds and love each other in order to defeat the evil spirits that are working in our families and churches. Evil spirits cannot do anything when we speak of love and comfort. You are making a mistake if you are not treating your spouse, children or fellow Christians with love, although you may emerge triumphant in the spiritual war. That is because evil spirits do not go away. They keep waiting for an opportunity to take advantage of your wounded emotions. You must remember that your spiritual power grows as your emotional wounds heal up. So see to it that your love for others keeps growing.

My Life and My Confession
Stories from the Mission Field
Jae-woong Cheon (missionary to Bolivia)

In 1995, I entered the sixth session of the mission training center of Korea Evangelical Holiness Church. After completing the training, I went to the Santa Cruise mission center in Bolivia. Bolivia was the poorest country in Latin America; drugs were overflowing along with extreme depravity. This was mainly because a month's wage was less than the minimum living costs for one family and jobs were limited. Also, corruption, depravity and mistrust were rampant in society. The depravity of Catholicism, the national religion (a combination of Virgin Mary worship and the local religion, which had taken the shape of holy virgin worship), had taken a heavy toll on the nation's spiritual life. Because of Catholicism, people were ignorant of the Bible and worshiped idols (holy virgin worship – holy virgin statues had been placed in every city and town). Demons were hard at work in Bolivia. In this mission field, God made me and my wife suffer hardships in order to turn us into His obedient servants and prayer warriors. During the training course, God gave us the power to cast out demons and to heal people.

Evil spirit of death and Emilene

Most of the Bolivians are Moreno (mix of Spanish white and Incan descendents). Indio is the next largest population, and blacks, who are despised and mistreated because of their appearance, constitute the smallest population in the country.

Emilene's mom was a Morena (male is called Moreno and female Morena) and her husband was black. Emilene's mom had three husbands and nine children. All three sons she had by her first husband went to prison for murder and robbery. She had a daughter by another husband. Her name was

Emilene and she grew up in an environment that was very close to sin. When she was 14 years old the demon of death entered her. One day, a few church members and I gathered at our church to visit her house at 8 o'clock in the evening. As Emilene did not want to join us she went to some other place and walked across the play ground next to our church. Satan worshippers regularly buried dead bodies in that playground. She heard someone calling her name from behind. She turned around and saw a man in black clothes. His eyes were red and he was calling her name. Emilene got scared and ran away. She said she did not remember what happened next.

All of us looked for her until midnight but we could not find her. Then a church member spotted Emilene. She was talking to someone on a side street. The member who saw her was a nurse. She checked Emilene's pulse and realised that the girl was not normal. Has she taken drugs? she wondered. The nurse took her back home. When they reached home Emilene could not recognise us and looked at us as if we were mad or something.

We placed Emilene in a room and waited for the effects of drugs to subside. Emilene asked me to turn off the light and I did so. But soon I found her talking to someone in the dark! I asked her who she was talking to and she said she was talking to two men in the room. Surprisingly, we could not see them. The moment I heard that, I knew that those two men were demons. Instantly, I cast them out in the name of Jesus. With a scream, Emilene vomited and spat out blood and when the nurse checked her pulse she found that the girl was absolutely normal.

Brother Juan and the Demon of Legion

Juan came to our church in order to destroy it. He lived together with our youth community. When we were attending our prayer meeting he suddenly twisted his body like a snake, breathed roughly and moaned strangely. I immediately knew that it was the work of a demon. I tried to cast the demon out in the name of Jesus but all in vain. Eight of our young men held his hands and feet but they also could not hold him down. The demon would just not leave Juan.

I asked the demon to tell me his name and he said that he was the demon of legion. When I asked him why he had taken possession of Juan he said that Juan was his. For three times during three years the demon of legion appeared in brother Juan. Our attempts to expel him from Juan's body proved abortive every time it appeared. The demon gradually lost its power in Juan, but never went out.

"After Jesus had gone indoors, his disciples asked him privately, 'Why couldn't we drive it out?' He replied, 'This kind can come out only by prayer' (Mark. 9:28-29). I prayed and fasted as the Bible said, but it was not enough. When I was trying to drive out the demon, Juan hit me hard with his open hand, sending me reeling backwards. I cried out to God, "Lord, I'll quit driving out demons if I fail to drive out the demon of legion in this brother. You said you'd give the power to drive out demons in the name of Jesus, but now I just can't do it. If I can't cast this demon out, then please take away my gift of casting out demons."

Then God said to me, "Get rid of his tattoo. The secret is in his tattoo." (Lev. 19:28 – Do not put tattoos on yourselves.) I asked Juan how he got his tattoo. It was his Satan-worshipping friend who had tattooed a skull with the devil's number 666 below it (Rev. 13). On his left arm, he had tattooed the god of alcohol. On the back there was a tattoo of sexual depravity and on his fingers there were tattoos of a demonic pattern and spells. I did not give much importance to tattoos. So I took Juan to a tattoo shop and got the skull on his right arm covered with the face of Jesus. The tattoo of the god of alcohol was big so I got it covered with a tattoo of the sun. The sexual depravity tattoo on his back was covered up by Jesus carrying the cross. The demonic patterns on his fingers were covered with the dove of the Holy Spirit. After that I asked Juan to repent for his sins in the name of Jesus. When We must remember that calling in demons is a sin and that demons come into our body through sin. It should also be noted that God wants us to be holy, that holiness, obedience and love go together and that holiness starts from obedience and is accomplished by love.

Chapter 9
What interrupts the fullness of the Holy Spirit?

Disobedience blocks your spiritual passage

The Holy Spirit grieves when we do not obey God, because the Holy Spirit is the spirit of God. This is why prophet Samuel said that obedience is better than sacrifice (1Sa. 15:22). God's Word is the promise and commandment. So when we obey the Word, God delights in us and when God is pleased with us, the Holy Spirit presides in us with power. Going to Sunday service and giving tithes to God is one of the commandments of God. Missing Sunday service for reasons such as conducting business, going for a picnic, watching TV, playing golf, and camping diminishes the presence of the Holy Spirit within you. Do not give a chance to evil spirits (Eph. 4:27). Go to church regularly and approach God with a sincere heart.

To give tithe is God's commandment and a way to be blessed (Deu. 14:22, Mal. 3:8). However, many spiritual beginners run into difficulties when it comes to giving tithe. They forget to give tithe or think about giving it but put it off until they miss the chance to give. This can be a serious problem if you are a person of the Holy Spirit. Pay tithe to

God come what may. If you miss the opportunity to pay tithe, you are likely to spend the money on some other things.

You make two mistakes when you do not give tithe. One is that you do not obey God's Word, and the other is that you reject being materially blessed by God. You face two more problems. Firstly, you give way to evil spirits because the presence of the Holy Spirit diminishes. Secondly, your financial inflow stops. The vicious cycle of spirit and material things begins. This vicious cycle can be broken only through repentance.

"Do not get drunk on wine" is a commandment of God (Jdg. 13:4, Eph. 5:18). Why does God hate liquor? Liquor makes us feel good, but only temporarily. By drinking we can forget our sadness and pains. Liquor pleases and frees our minds. It makes us brave by covering up our shame. It heats up our body. Yes, what liquor does for us is so similar to what the Holy Spirit does for us. This is why people in the book of Acts said that those who were in fullness of the Holy Spirit were drunk in new wine.

In the past and even now, people replace God with liquor. "What's the big deal about having a pint of beer?" You may refute. Be that as it may, if you cannot cut off what is connected to drinking beer, evil spirits will do serious harm to you. My high school history teacher was a heavy drinker and he always said this in classes: "First, I drink the liquor. Next, liquor drinks liquor. And finally, liquor drinks me." Nowadays people soothe their hidden religiousness with liquor. Anyway, it is clear that the Holy Spirit worries about us when we get drunk.

Church members must heed the words of their pastor, because a pastor proclaims the Word of God and wields the spiritual authority given by God. Male believers often fail to heed the words of their pastor. Given below is a typical train of thought.

What is the difference between a pastor and me?
He is not even older than me!
He is not better than me in anything!
He is just an ordinary man!

You must not forget that it was God who wanted you "to recognise those who labour among you, and are over you in the Lord and admonish you, and esteem them very highly in love for their work's sake (1Th. 5:12-13). You may be better than your pastor in many respects, but you should never look down upon him. If you respect your pastor, your life will move forward smoothly. I want all Christians to respect their pastors and consequently enjoy a healthy and blessed religious life.

I think the mother of Rockefeller, the richest person in the 20th century, knew these spiritual secrets. She told her son about ten disciplines. They are:

1. Serve God as you serve your father.
2. Serve and assist your pastor next to God.
3. Attend Sunday service in your church.
4. Always leave your right pocket for tithe.
5. Do not make enemies of anyone.
6. Set up daily goals and plans in the morning and pray for them.
7. Look into yourself, repent and give prayers of hope before going to bed.
8. Reading the Bible and meditating on it is the first thing you do in the morning.
9. Help your neighbors as best as you can.
10. Sit in the front row at worship services.

Throughout his life, Rockefeller religiously followed his mother's lessons and eventually he enjoyed the blessing of God.

Do not stand against your pastor! If you do, you will have difficulties like the descendants of Korah (Num. 16:1-35). If you cannot trust your pastor, then you should try not to see him as much as you can, but you must pray for him. Never say bad things about the pastor to other believers. He was chosen by God (Num. 12:1-16). We cannot judge our pastors. Only God can judge them. We have to accept the sovereignty of God. Therefore, accept God! Do not wait for God to judge your pastor. Pray for him with tears instead. God not only receives your prayer, but also delights in you. The God of the Holy Spirit will pour out blessings upon you and your children if you do that. Do not block your spiritual passage because of your relationship with your pastor.

Doubt and fear weaken our faith

As children of God, we received God's promise of blessings. But evil spirits make us doubt the promise (Gen. 3:1). Think about the Israelites who were turning around Jericho with faith in order to go to Canaan, the Promised Land. They might have turned around first through the third day with steadfast faith and confidence. However, on the fourth day, they might have doubted a little and on the fifth day they might have started to worry about it.

"What if that solid Jericho never falls down?"

The sixth day came and they might have been in fear. The King and soldiers of Jericho might have laughed at the Israelites. However, on the last day they might have turned around because they did not have any other choice. And the people of Jericho might have watched them going in suspicion. It is clear that doubt swallows up our faith (Jam. 1:6-7). Therefore, we should drive away our doubts while waiting for God's promise to be achieved. It is evident that a doubtful mind continues to grow in fear. The evil spirit comes with fear to those who doubt the promise of God. The moment we doubt God's love or the work of the Holy Spirit, the Spirit inside us grieves. Evil spirits expand their territory where there is doubt and at the same time the work of the Holy Spirit shrinks.

There was a sister who ran a flower garden and did floral arrangements in our church. This faithful young woman was a choir member and attended Yoido Full Gospel Church. One day she came to our church at night to do some flower arrangement and incidentally attended our prayer meeting. We talked during the meeting and I heard how the sister had lost her gift of tongues. A few years ago her friend, who was in the army, came out for a recess. They met and had dinner together. While having dinner her friend said to her, "What do you mean by speaking in tongues in these modern days! That's just one of the mental phenomena. People praying in tongues look crazy."

She carefully listened to what he said and eventually started to doubt her gift, regarding it as worthless. Strangely, she lost her gift of tongues soon after she harboured such thoughts. I told her to repent for doubting the Holy Spirit and thinking low of the gift. So she prayed and repented, and her tongues burst out again. Truly, the Holy Spirit does not stay inside those who are given to doubting.

How can we overcome disbelief and fear? We should gather and pray together. My own faith may be weak, but when we pray together, strangely, our faith becomes stronger.

One day, in July of 2002, I made up my mind to plant a church. I did not volunteer for the planting of the church, but I saw the providence and guidance of God. So I chose to take a bold step. But then, I did not have any money, and there was no one to help me in the planting of the church. However, I firmly believed that it was what God wanted— that I should plant a church.

What interrupts the fullness of the Holy Spirit?

One week had passed since I made up my mind to plant a church. Deacon Shin, who just had moved into Seoul from Jecheon, called me. I regarded that call as a call made by God, so I asked him to help me in planting a church. But he hesitated. So I suggested, "Please come and pray with me just for a few months and help me in planting a church." He agreed and I started looking for a building for rent. It was not easy to find such a building. But I believed in God's promise and I signed a contract for an apartment storeroom in a new downtown area in Bucheon. That storeroom already had facilities that were necessary for a church. Since I had no money, I had no other option. So I just made a temporary contract with the condition of placing a deposit of 20 million won and 1 million won as monthly rent. First, I paid the deposit of 300 thousand won by credit card loan. I did not know from where my faith came.

Then I started to pray every night at 8 o'clock with my wife and Deacon Shin at the place we had rented. We anxiously prayed together in tongues. While we prayed, owners of the Chinese restaurant and the laundry, which were next to our place, and the building manager came to see us. They asked us who we were and why we were so noisy, praying in a strange language. The owner of the Chinese restaurant concluded that we were heretics. I explained to them that we were the people who would soon sign the contract for the storeroom and that we were not heretics. Few days later, I signed an official contract. I took another loan for 2.7 million won and paid the contract deposit. And then suddenly doubt and fear covered me.

"What am I supposed to do if I can't get 20 million won for the deposit?"

I went there to pray every single night and it took me 20 minutes to walk from Bucheon Jungdong subway station. I was not even tired. I was not tired because I felt that I could not bear the doubt and fear if I did not pray. I was calm and peaceful while praying at night. But sometimes I blamed myself for signing a contract for such an expensive place without having any plans. My heart shriveled every time I thought about it. However, the die had been cast. Regret was of no use. I had to move on. If not, I would waste the contract deposit and fall deep into despair. Deacon Shin's sister joined our evening prayer. We prayed together desperately. We prayed in that manner until the night of July 31st. Then I decided to fast and pray from August 1st until the 15th, which was the date on which I had to pay the rest of the contract deposit. And on the same night, Deacon Shin also made the same decision to pray and fast in the morning from August 1st to 15th. I was glad to hear that. My faith deepened when I thought, "The Holy Spirit is giving us the same heart." So we gathered at the place and fasted and prayed for two to three hours, and while we prayed we received heavenly peace in our hearts.

While we were continuing our prayer we heard from Deacon Shin that Deaconess Son had moved to Gwacheon from Jechoen. Actually I had nothing to do with the believers in Jecheon, but while I was in the army, my wife led the prayer meeting several times there. It was really the amazing providence of God. Deaconess Son had to come to Seoul because her husband was suffering from lung cancer. Anyway, we visited her house and prayed together. The next thing I had to do was to look for the deposit for the church. However, twice, the bank loan attempts failed and I felt like I was standing at the edge of a cliff. There was nothing I could do except fasting and praying together with people. I had to do that because if I had not, I might have lost my faith with the tides of disbelief. As I was desperately praying, God allowed me to get the bank loan on August 14th, just one day before the payment day. "Thank you God!" I shouted. "Now, we will start with our faith." My faith towards church planting started to deepen.

The Bible tells us to gather together in order to overcome our doubts. We have to get together as much as we can. We must come to the worship service regularly to enjoy the grace of God. If not, our faith will disappear and doubt and fear will appear. We also have to memorise and meditate on the word of God.

"Do not let your hearts be troubled. Trust in God; trust also in me." (Jn. 14:1).

"Now faith is being sure of what we hope for and certain of what we do not see."(Heb. 11:1).

"Fear not, for I have redeemed you; I have summoned you by name; you are mine." (Isa. 43:1).

We have to defeat our disbelief and fear with the Word of God (Mt. 4:1-11). We have to use the name of Jesus Christ to defeat it (Gal. 6:17). If not, our spirit will be caught by evil spirits. The Holy Spirit comes with power to those who accept God with faith and hope (Heb. 11:6).

An arrogant person denies god

An arrogant person does not believe in God. Some people seem to be modest and polite, but are in actuality rather arrogant. On the other hand, there are those who may seem to be arrogant and proud, but who are in actuality extremely loyal to God.

The Holy Spirit stays closer to those who fear God. Some believers are rather harsh to God. They are sensitive to other people's feelings but do not mind being harsh to God. What they do not realise is the fact that there is no point in being sensitive to other people's feelings if we do not follow the Word of God. That is a snare (Pro. 29:25). King Saul failed because he did not fear God. He feared his people too much (1Sam. 15:24-31). The Bible says that the Spirit of the Lord departed from Saul, and a distressing spirit from the Lord troubled him (1Sam. 16:14).

We fear people too much. We worry about what they will think about us. I sometimes get disappointed at myself whenever I fear other people. Our faith naturally weakens when we fear other people too much. We have to fear God instead of other people. It is from God that we receive the real salvation (Isa. 31:1-3). David became a great King because he always thought about God in every situation (1Sam. 24:1-7). He truly knew the secret of humility.

Also, an arrogant person does not accept his own limitations. The Bible tells us that humans are incapable and evil. However, arrogant people rely more on their ability and personality rather than on God's power. There are Christians who indirectly show off their righteousness. They claim that they are saved by God's grace and that they stand before God with this merit. But their heart is filled with pride and confidence in their own merit or behavior. God hates such arrogant people. The Holy Spirit does not come to these people.

Therefore, true modesty is all about acknowledging God's authority and rule, in every single moment. Humility is about admitting that our life belongs to God and giving our life to God when He asks for it. On the contrary, an arrogant person never accepts God as master and therefore gives nothing to Him. God refuses the arrogant. And the Spirit of the Lord comes to those who are humble (Pro. 3:34).

Spiritual and physical health care

Christianity, which inclines towards asceticism, has always regarded the human body as a kind of prison for the spirit and soul. Enjoying physical pleasure was thus condemned, and the human body was mistreated. Only the spirit was regarded as precious. But this is where the problem lies. The body cannot be regarded as something worthless, for had the body been worthless, God would not have given it to us. Just like the spirit, our body is also important. The body is not a prison for the spirit and soul. It is a vessel meant to serve the spirit and soul.

When I was in Korea I just could not stop playing tennis. I normally played too much and too hard before I went to attend the evening prayer meeting. I found it rather difficult to pray well because of tiredness. As a result, my communication with the Holy Spirit weakened considerably. Also, my voice got too hoarse. I could not deliver God's grace to fellow believers, although I prayed really hard. Our body is a means of delivering and receiving spiritual grace. Although our spirit is more important than our body, all our spiritual goods become valueless if our body is not in its normal state. We must therefore value our body in order to receive the grace of the Holy Spirit.

However, this does not mean that we should value our body more than our spirit and soul. We should give top priority to spiritual development and, at the same time, not disregard our physical being, mainly because we need physical health in order to be in the fullness of the Holy Spirit. We should go jogging to pray hard and to be loyal to God. If necessary, we should take rest in the afternoon so that we could pray at night and in the early morning. We should eat well in order to pray hard. God provided food through a crow and through an angel to Elijah, who got exhausted

(1Ki. 17:2-7, 19:4-8). We should know that our spirit will break down when our body, our vessel, is broken. Likewise, our body is healthy when our soul is healthy. This is why mind control or positive thinking is so important. Our soul can affect our spirit and body. I learned that as a pastor, watching too much television before preaching made my sermon less graceful. We should thus control our TV-watching time and keep away from things that dim our soul.

Evil spirits have many ways to hunt down and harass our soul. Sometimes, they try to capture our mind through popular culture. So we need to be careful not to become a victim of popular culture. We should take cognizance of only the positive aspects of popular culture.

Briefly, we need to take good care of our spirit, soul and body so that our spirit is always ready to effectively communicate with the Holy Spirit and that we are always in a position to maintain the fullness of the Spirit.

My Life and My Confession

I am a Happy Person
Shin-young Kim (Executive of Paul Media)

There was a man in Korea who had lost both his parents. His mother always went to a Buddhist temple to pray whenever his father's business was bad or her children had to take a national examination for university entrance. His brothers, who grew up under the same parents, were also atheists. This man's father lived a busy life, working for his personal business. His wife also used to go to a Buddhist temple and was the member of a Buddhist club before she married him. They were not rich, but happy. Then one day, his wife started to go to church led by the mother of her son's friend. Her husband did not take it seriously because many people went to church and it was not bad to have a religion. His wife became a positive person since she started to go to church and it seemed that she well endured difficulties, so he thought it was better than before. But it was more than that.

Her husband was running a personal business. Unexpectedly, the business started to wane when his wife started to go to church. Because the place where he was living had to be reconstructed, he had to move to a place called Bucheon in Kyounggido, a place he had never heard about before. But his work place was in Seoul, so it was not easy for him to commute.

His wife attended a small church that had just been planted. On Sundays, the husband stayed home alone and his wife went to church with their children. Moreover, she went to church on weekdays and came back late after praying at church. One day her husband got mad and said, "Why is a housewife always coming home late at night?" But his wife said, "I'm doing it for the happiness of our family." He was shocked by her answer. A housewife going out at night for the happiness of a family? Is she practising some kind of a strange religion? They had a fight over this issue, and that day the husband forced his wife to stay at home.

Then his wife cried out loud. So he met the church pastor and asked, "Why do this church's people gather at night?" "Isn't religion a kind of a mind-control process to get peace of mind?" "Aren't Buddha and Jesus almost the same?" The pastor said, "Well, it is natural that you think that way. But…"

From that day on, the husband started to study Christianity by first studying 'The Collapse of Theory of Evolution," which the pastor had asked him to consider. He was an atheist and he read the whole Bible during his commute to his workplace and home. He read books that criticised

Christianity and many Christian testimonies and books of apologetics. Every Saturday, he debated with the pastor until 2 o'clock to 3 o'clock in the morning. He was an atheist and he lived like that for more than six months.

When he was doing that he started to attend church with his wife. There were only about ten church members. He thought it was pathetic. It was just a small church. One day a praise leader did not come, so the pastor asked him to play the guitar because he was part of the music industry. He played unwillingly. His performance was well appreciated. Another day, the piano player did not come, so he had to play the piano. His performance was appreciated yet again. A few days later, the piano player moved away and had to attend another church. Eventually, a non-believer with no faith became a church piano player.

"What am I doing here? I don't believe in this religion. So why am I doing all this?" he kept asking himself. He thought he had taken a strange responsibility. And he had done it because the people in the church liked him and the little church needed him.

His business got even worse, but his interest in Christianity grew. Eventually, he failed in his business. He started another small business in a new place. "Oh! Nothing is working out right ever since I started going to church. This is terrible!" He muttered.

Although he was impressed with Christianity, he did not fully believe in it. He read a book titled *Daring to Live on the Edge* and memorised some parts of it. "This really is a good book. I think all Christians should memorise it."

He recalled the contents of the book on his way back home. And suddenly he recalled all of the mistakes he had made and the sins he had committed in the past. He just could not hold back his tears. He cried for thirty minutes while driving back home. Although he wept, he felt a strange happiness welling up in his heart. "The pastor was right. This world was truly created by God. Oh, I should have known about God earlier. I'm really a sinner!" The most surprising thing on earth had happened to him. "Thank you Lord. Thank you for calling a sinner like me. It was all part of your wonderful plan: my wife's going to church, my failing in business, my meeting with Pastor Jung... Thank you so much Lord."

Since then he has been trying hard to live a proper Christian life. He is now trying hard to make his parents practice Christianity and is working in a church as a piano player and a praise leader. He runs his business for God's glory. His children's education is based on the Bible, and his wife, who serves at a church kitchen, receives counseling education. Both of them are earnestly working for the happiness of their family and the welfare of their church.

He loves to sing a song that goes like this:

> My God, my God, my God, who is with me.
>
> Father, Father, Father, who called a sinner.
>
> Thank you. Thank you. I give my life for you.

Lord what made you call a sinner like me? he still wonders. And he says:

> You only know my way. Lead me Lord. Yes, I am that husband.
>
> I'm so happy to be with my wife.
>
> I'm so happy to have lovely children.
>
> I'm so happy to meet a good pastor.

I'm so happy to grow along with a beautiful church. Most of all, I'm so thankful that I am with God.

I'm so happy a person.

Chapter 10
Keeping the fullness of the Holy Spirit

Repent

Repentance is the first step to being in the fullness of the Holy Spirit. We have to repent at all times, not because we committed a sin, but because we are born as sinners. It is just like taking bath frequently. No matter how clean we are after taking a bath, we get dirty again because of sweat and dirt. It is just the same. Our sins were washed away by the blood of Jesus when we accepted Jesus as our savior. However, because of the original sin that remains in us, we are tempted by sin and we commit sin again and again through our thoughts and actions.

Therefore, we have to wash our spirit with the blood of Jesus before we come to God. Repentance is an essential step towards coming closer to God. God is pleased by our repentance and contrition (Ps. 34:18, Ps. 51:17 and Isa. 57:15) because He is holy. We see the presence of the Holy Spirit in the power within us after we wash away our sins with the blood of Jesus. Therefore, repentance is something that only Christians can do. Repentance is the right tool for receiving the saving grace of God. We need to repent and sing songs praising the Blood of Jesus in order to be filled with the Holy Spirit. This is the only way of preventing evil sprits from taking possession of us. (Gal. 6:17).

Forgive

God forgives our sins through the blood of Jesus. We should also forgive those who have done wrong to us (Col. 3:13). If we do not forgive them, God will ask us of our sins (Mt. 6:14-15). Forgiving others is a proof of God's forgiveness.

Most people have someone in their heart they could never forgive. Some say they cannot forgive their father for abusing them in their childhood, while others say they cannot forgive their mother for loving their brother more than them. And some say they cannot forgive their brothers and sisters for disregarding or trampling over them over.

The Bible says, 'Man's enemies are the members of his own household' (Mic. 7:6, Mt. 10:36). How true! Many female Christians fail to forgive their husbands for making them suffer—so overwhelming is their hatred for their husbands God's love or forgiveness is far away from them whenever hatred overwhelms them. Husbands retaliate by saying they are not happy with their wives.

Where would the enemy of a Christian be? I think our enemy is in our church. I heard a believer say that he did not want to go to church because he hated somebody in the church. Hatred for someone diminishes the presence of the Holy Spirit. God is love and He cannot come to a person who hates other people.

One night, my wife and I were praying and one fellow believer came to us unexpectedly. She wanted to talk to us, so we talked for several hours. She really wanted to believe in Jesus and wanted her life to be changed. But it was not easy.

She said depression and sadness always reigned over her. While she was telling us her story, she confessed that she could not forgive her mother who had left her when she was young. After few hours of consultation, she made up her mind to forgive her mother. Her life began to change drastically soon after she forgave her mother. I could see the Holy Spirit working in her life. Forgiveness is an act of great faith.

If you really want to be filled with the Holy Spirit, forgive someone you hate, for you also will be forgiven! Do that and all the pain in you will be gone and the grace of the Holy Spirit will flourish within you. Forgiveness enables us to achieve the fullness of the Spirit.

Keep the Word of God

The Bible is the word of God. Through the word of God we can communicate with the Holy Spirit. Meditating and memorising God's word is a short cut to becoming intimate with the Holy Spirit. If we fill our thoughts with the word of God, the Holy Spirit will become friendlier. Watching television or reading potboilers will make our thoughts rather complicated. How can the Holy Spirit stay within us if our thoughts are full of scary movies or pornographic rubbish? TV programs or novels are useful as long as they help us in reducing depression. However, we must purify our mind and soul with the word of God after taking our share of life's enjoyments The Holy Spirit will be pleased with us if we open up our Bibles instead of the newspaper in the morning. Then we can go into the world with confidence and take what is appropriate for us. Before we go to bed, we should again purify our spirit and soul with God's word.

Benefits of gathering

In order to receive God's grace, we need to get together in one place. "When the day of Pentecost came, they were all together in one place" (Acts. 2:1). Jesus and his disciples and other followers got together at all times (Act. 1:13, 15). When we gather, we see the word of God. It is more effective when we gather together more often. This is why evil spirits try hard to interrupt people's gatherings. When the Israelites were in despair under the threat of the Philistines, Samuel called all the Israelites to Mizpah. There they fasted and cried out to the Lord. (1Sam. 7:5-6).

The writer of the Epistle to the Hebrews said, "Let us not give up meeting together, as some are in the habit of doing, but let us encourage one another all the more as you see the Day approaching." Therefore, we must all attend official services and frequently attend prayer meetings. The presence of the Holy Spirit will be felt more powerfully in a gathering because we are all spiritual beings. Jesus said, "For where two or three come together in my name, there am I with them" (Mt. 18:20).

It should be noted that those who do not miss prayer meetings find it easy to come to prayer meetings, but those who often miss prayer meetings find it hard to attend them. It has also been observed that those who do not attend prayer meetings regularly often encounter obstacles to attending prayer meetings: They sprain their ankle, their contract strangely fails or their children would not listen to them. Such people blame one another for their inability to attend prayer meetings. Somehow they manage to come to a prayer meeting. Perhaps this is the spiritual law for the people of God. Thus the writer of Hebrews says:

"And you have forgotten that word of encouragement that addresses you as sons: 'My son, do not make light of the Lord's discipline, and do not lose heart when he rebukes you' (Heb. 12:5).

"Because the Lord disciplines those he loves, and he punishes everyone he accepts as a son" (Heb. 12:6).

"Endure hardship as discipline; God is treating you as sons. For what son is not disciplined by his father?" (Heb. 12: 7).

"If you are not disciplined (and everyone undergoes discipline), then you are illegitimate children and not true sons" (Heb. 12:8).

"Moreover, we have all had human fathers who disciplined us and we respected them for it. How much more should we submit to the Father of our spirits and live!" (Heb. 12:9).

"Our fathers disciplined us for a little while as they thought best; but God disciplines us for our good, that we may share in his holiness" (Heb. 12:10).

When a believer is spiritually oppressed, a pastor intercedes for him. The pastor tries to untangle what is spiritually tied up. Sometimes the pastor complains, "Wait a minute! It's they who troubled their spirit because there were not awake. Why do I have to be responsible for it?" But soon the pastor realises that God has entrusted him with the responsibility.

We have to attend official services. We have to attend prayer meetings faithfully. In conclusion, we should never give any chance to evil spirits. Didn't Jesus say "stay awake and pray so that we won't be tempted"? Do not think that you could get away easily after giving a chance to evil spirits. A small crack can destroy a huge dam.

Join the prayer

Acts 1:14 says that the disciples of Jesus joined together for prayer. Act. 2:46 says, "Every day they continued to meet together in the temple courts." The Holy Spirit is the spirit that makes us become one. Therefore it is very important to pray together. We cannot fail to feel the powerful presence of the Spirit if we pray together every day. Heaven's doors will open if we pray for the same thing with one accord. If you share your prayer with your brothers and sisters in Christ, you will get faster answers from God.

When I was about to publish the book *Meeting Jesus!*, I was seriously worrying about the color of the border of the book cover. So I prayed for it with church members. One day, during the prayer meeting, people who were praying all together said 'white.' A white border was thus added to the cover of *Meeting Jesus!* And the cover really looked beautiful.

Evil spirits try to split gatherings. Although people gather in one place, they are not of one mind. A pastor or a believer says something, and people misunderstand the message. If that is the case, we should speak little and sing more praises of repentance instead. We should wage a spiritual war against evil spirits. And we must sincerely fast and pray. Peace will come to us again once we defeat evil spirits.

Fast and pray

Sometimes when we pray we feel that God is not with us anymore. In such a situation, fasting and praying could be very effective and powerful.

Great leaders in the Bible knew about the power of fasting and praying. Moses, Samuel, David and Esther sought God through the fasting prayer and received answers. Moses is probably the first person to fast and pray for 40 days. Well I have not fasted for more than 2 to 3 days. But God values even short-term fasting and responds to it without fail.

It seems that Sung-su Park, the owner of Korea's representative Christian enterprise E-Land, knew well about the power of fasting prayer. According to his testimony, he fasted and prayed to God whenever there were big problems.

He fasted and prayed during the crisis of dishonor in IMF, 1998, and God dramatically saved his company. American Bank brought $500 million and chose 10 blue chip companies in Korea to invest and E-Land was one among the ten. Behind this miracle, was Park's fasting prayer.

Recently, the news of E-Land buying Carrefour was one of the main topics of discussion in the financial world. It was something that never could have happened. E-Mart and Samsung Home-plus were the most competitive supermarkets, but E-Land, which was the smallest, succeeded in purchasing Carrefour. Sung-su Park announced that out of the profit that would be gained through purchasing Carrefour, 100 billion won will be used for North Korean brothers and needy people. At 'The 20th anniversary discipleship training leadership seminar' held in June 2006 at Sarang Community Church, Park gave a testimony that he fasted four times during the process of Car-fu purchasing. As the head of the E-Land enterprise, he confessed that the strength behind Car-fu purchase was trust in God and the power of prayer.

When we fast and pray we are filled with the Holy Spirit. Our sinful desires disappear and we become spiritual persons. We do feel hungry and tired often. Whenever we feel these things the Holy Spirit lessens our physical pains. This is the story of Pastor Jun-gon Kim, the chairman of Korea CCC, when he fasted for 40 days. Pastor Kim was very hungry and he could not bear the hunger. All of a sudden he caught a whiff of noodles. And then a strange thing happened. He became full and the gnawing pangs of hunger disappeared. It was the Holy Spirit that had helped him.

Some time ago, four of our church members went to Osanli Prayer Meeting and fasted for four days. One of them was a new convert. He used to be very critical of Christianity before he became a Christian. So it was really difficult for him to adapt himself to the atmosphere of prayer. Everyone, to him, looked crazy. It was the same on the following day. Moreover, hunger and cold had frozen up his mind. But there was no transportation to come down the mountain, so unwillingly he had to stay there. On the last day, a strange thing happened to him. His spiritual eyes had opened. On the first day everyone had looked crazy to him, but now they all appeared to be normal. Also, he felt that people were becoming more familiar to him. People who played the guitar and led the praise seemed so beautiful to him. He also started believing in Jesus. Certainly, fasting prayer enables us to feel the presence of the Holy Spirit in our life.

Cautions for fasting

There are some people who do fasting prayer improperly. They fast and pray too often. They fast without a plan. Some people fast in the morning for 100 days. I am of the opinion that fasting is easier and full of grace when it is based on God's plan. God tells us when to start fasting.

We should fast when God wants us to fast and when God helps our fasting. There will be side effects when we fast and pray according to our own plan. We must remember that improper fasting, being obsessed with fasting and obsolete 100 days of morning fasting actually produce no results. They will only ruin our health. Also, as a result of our fasting, evil spirits may start using us as their weapon.

Consult your family members and pastor before you start your 40-day long fasting. Of course, it is you who decides whether you will start fasting or not. But you should not make your wife and pastor feel that you are fasting for an improper reason. Fasting to escape from your problems and difficulties is also not an appropriate way of fasting. Therefore, you must fast only when God wants you to fast.

When you fast, both the Holy Spirit and evil spirits become active in your life. Evil spirits do not want you to go closer to God, so they start tempting you in subtle ways. Let us say, you start fasting after a long time. Quite unexpectedly, someone who has not been really kind to you gives you a snack or a chewing gum. You unconsciously take it and eat it. And then, much to your horror, you realise that you have broken your fast unwittingly. It was an evil spirit that came to you in the form of that person. If you find yourself in a similar situation, do not panic, for God is aware of your innermost intentions. Try not to feel guilty about breaking your fast. A guilty conscience is what the evil spirit wants. God is not narrow-minded. Remember that what matters to God is not your commitment, but your repentance.

Epilogue

The Holy Spirit enables us to lead a vibrant life
The Holy Spirit provides us with immense joy and peace. "The mind of a sinful man is death, but the mind controlled by the Spirit is life and peace" (Rom. 8:6). When the Holy Spirit leads us, children prophesy, young men see visions and old men have dreams according to what is written in Ezekiel—we experience mystical gifts and miracles of the Holy Spirit.

Your relationship with God comes first
We must not forget that wonderful gifts of the Holy Spirit are given to Christians to comfort weak believers and to build up churches. The gifts should not be used for building up *your* authority over other believers. If you become arrogant, God will chastise you and you may become a weapon of evil spirits. Therefore, those who have received the gift of the Holy Spirit must seek to bear the fruits of the Holy Spirit.

Also, our dream, vision and prophecy cannot change God's plan. They tell us in advance about what God intends to do. If we are swayed by the gift, we may follow the person with the gift and ignore the Holy Spirit. As recipients of the gift of the Holy Spirit, we must invite Jesus to enter our life. We must attach more importance to our relationship with God rather than to the gifts of the Holy Spirit. Also, we must always try to be with God. The gift of the Holy Spirit will come naturally to us if we are in Jesus and Jesus is in us. Anyone who abides in Christ will naturally bear the fruit of the Holy Spirit (Jn. 15:5-8).

The Holy Spirit extends our boundary

The Holy Spirit sometimes enables us to perform even those tasks that we consider impossible. Acts 1:8 says, "But you will receive power when the Holy Spirit comes on you; and you will be my witnesses in Jerusalem, and in all Judea and Samaria, and to the ends of the earth."

The disciples' vision was limited to Jerusalem and Judea. Also, their imagination could not go beyond Samaria. But Jesus said, "When the Holy Spirit comes, his power will break through your limitation and will stretch the boundary of your vision to reach the ends of the earth."

To Nicodemus, Jesus gave a new definition of 'ends of the earth.' "The wind blows wherever it pleases. You hear its sound, but you cannot tell where it comes from or where it is going. So it is with everyone born of the Spirit" (Jn. 3:8). People of the Holy Spirit will discover new visions, new ends of the earth and a new blue ocean; they will see things they have not seen before.

Christianity is a vibrant religion because the Holy Spirit is alive. The Holy Spirit will speak to us every moment and every day to lead us to believe in Jesus. It is the Holy Spirit who gave us the vision to embrace the world and who made the vision possible for D.L. Moody, who was a mere cobbler. The life of those who listen to the voice of the Holy Spirit is one big adventure.

The Holy Spirit adds genuineness to a church
What is the meaning of the phrase "a church becoming a church in the Holy Spirit"?

Firstly, it means that a church becomes a genuine church when the Holy Spirit begins to reside in it. The Holy Spirit enables Christians to feel the presence of God and unites them in God's grace.

Suppose you are attending a church service. The service leader asks you to open the Bible at 2Kings chapter 16. You get a surprise when you learn that you have already opened your Bible at chapter 16. Consider another scenario: You are touched by the Holy Spirit when you read Psalms 23:1-6 at your home. After reading the verses, you attend an evening service. You are taken aback by the fact that the preacher's sermon is based on the verses you read at home. In the second scenario, Psalms 23:1-6 is the voice of the Holy Spirit. Consider yet another scenario: While attending a church service you want to sing hymn number 123. Surprisingly, the worship leader or piano player asks the congregation to stand and sing the same hymn. These scenarios are convincing enough, and some of us may have actually encountered them in our lives. They all draw our attention to the fact that the Holy Spirit is always active.

Secondly, the phrase "a church becoming a church in the Holy Spirit" means that the Church gives us hope and love—things that the world lacks. The Church is the 'only hope' and its presence constantly underscores God's love for us.

After resurrection, Jesus asks Peter, who had denied Him earlier, a heart-piercing question: "Simon, son of Jonah, do you love me more than these?" Jesus knows the limitation of the love that a human being has. It is by the power of the Holy Spirit that we should love the world. Only then the world will understand and feel God's love for humans.

The Holy Spirit helps us to come together in harmony by fostering love amongst us. People of the Holy Spirit are like bridge makers. They build bridges between people.

Believing in Jesus through the Holy Spirit

I wrote this book to bring all Christians closer to God and to motivate them to become witnesses of Jesus through the Holy Spirit. We can testify God's love for us only when we are in the fullness of the Holy Spirit. Also, we become witnesses of the gospel and martyrs when we are filled with the Spirit (Act. 1:8).

It is important to obtain a deep theological insight into the presence of the Holy Spirit and the gifts and fruits of the Holy Spirit.

Come closer to the Holy Spirit and be guided by Him — this is what Jesus wants us to do. Jesus said that the Holy Spirit would come only when He leaves his disciples and goes to the Father. Jesus announced the beginning of the age of the Holy Spirit to us. The Holy Spirit works to fulfill the remaining task of Jesus. We are now living in a new age — an age that requires us to have new power and employ new methods.

Walking with the Holy Spirit brings joy and happiness. We pray for a sick person's recovery, and the evil spirit of disease retreats. We pray for the right direction, and the Spirit guides our life's course. We pray when our hearts are heavy, and the Holy Spirit gives us amazing peace. The Holy Spirit transforms a church into a genuine church. Even a poor family can experience immense joy through the Holy Spirit.

Our prayer becomes really powerful in the presence of the Holy Spirit. We need the Holy Spirit when we sing praises to the Lord, for the Spirit lends extraordinary power to our voice and heart. The presence of the Holy Spirit gives us joy and hope and makes our lives vibrant.

> I'm rejoicing night and day, as I walk the pilgrim way,
> For the hand of God in all my life I see,
> And the reason of my bliss, Yes, the secret all is this:
> That the Comforter abides with me.
> He abides, He abides, Hallelujah, He abides with me!
> I'm rejoicing night and day, as I walk the narrow way,
> For the Comforter abides with me.

www.ingramcontent.com/pod-product-compliance
Lightning Source LLC
Chambersburg PA
CBHW022133080426
42734CB00006B/338